DATE DUE

APR 26 1988		

CONSUMER SPATIAL BEHAVIOUR

CONSUMER SPATIAL BEHAVIOUR

A Model of Purchasing Decisions over Space and Time

ROBERT W. BACON

CLARENDON PRESS · OXFORD
1984

Oxford University Press, Walton Street, Oxford OX2 6DP
London New York Toronto
Delhi Bombay Calcutta Madras Karachi
Kuala Lumpur Singapore Hong Kong Tokyo
Nairobi Dar es Salaam Cape Town
Melbourne Auckland
and associated companies in
Beirut Berlin Ibadan Mexico City Nicosia

Oxford is a trade mark of Oxford University Press

Published in the United States
by Oxford University Press, New York

British Library Cataloguing in Publication Data

Bacon, Robert W.
Consumer spatial behaviour.
1. Consumers—Mathematical models
2. Geography, Economic—Mathematical models
I. Title
318'.3   HB820

ISBN 0-19-828476-4

Set by DMB (Typesetting), Oxford
Printed in Great Britain by
The Alden Press, Oxford

For
HARIKLEIA

PREFACE

I have been interested in the spatial choice aspect of consumer behaviour ever since I investigated, as a student, the patterns of shopping at a centre in the suburbs of Oxford. Some of the empirical material of that investigation was published in *The Cowley Shopping Centre* (1968). The study of the individual households using that centre convinced me that I did not have an adequate conceptual model to understand the choice between centres made for different goods by the various families surveyed. In particular, I was struck by the differences in frequencies exhibited in the purchase of common goods and accordingly I developed a model (Bacon (1971)) to show how to optimize between locations offering different ranges of goods when the frequencies of shopping were different. I attempted at that time to generalize the model to the case where there were price differentials between centres, but was unable to do so even after seeing Evans's (1972) elegant reformulation of my model as a linear programme. In the next decade I returned to the same on other occasions, but with the same result in each case. However, in 1981 I read a pre-publication version of the paper by Eaton and Lipsey (1982) which, although concentrating on the supply side, had a demand side related to my theoretical paper. The interest that this kindled was sufficient to allow the solution of the 'price differential model', and then the development of the other parts of the book followed.

My intellectual debt is, then, directly to those who have worked in this field in the last decade, and I hope that I have adequately indicated the key papers in the text. I have also benefited greatly from my discussions over the years with Donald Hay. His interest in the problem and his willingness to read and comment on what I have written have been an important factor in the production of this book.

I owe a debt of a different kind to my family who, during this period, have had to contend not only with the writing of this book but with the construction of houses. I hope the completion of both will justify their forbearance.

CONTENTS

Contents ix

LIST OF FIGURES

LIST OF TABLES

1

INTRODUCTION

The purpose of this book is to lay the foundations for the study of spatial consumer theory, and in so doing to resolve certain difficulties and to fill some of the gaps in that area of knowledge where urban geography and consumer economics overlap.

The primary question to which an answer is sought is this: what determines the choice of locations at which a given consumer will purchase the goods that are subsequently consumed? We can imagine a consumer located at a certain point in a town, with a given income, a family of given size, etc., and facing a choice between possible locations for buying all the goods that will be required. There may be an urban centre providing all types of shops, a few smaller suburban centres which are each made up of a substantial (and probably similar) range of shops, and many clusters of neighbourhood or local centres (ranging in size from one to a handful of shops). Economic theory, which has a great deal to say about patterns of expenditure on the different goods (demand theory), has surprisingly little to say about the factors governing where the goods will be bought, and so this question can be regarded as of intellectual interest in its own right. Also, once a model of individual consumer behaviour has been established, we can then aggregate over all the consumers in the town and derive the 'market areas' of the different shops and shopping centres. The study of market areas has received a large amount of attention but the models used, for example the 'gravity' model of Reilly (1931), are purely aggregative or statistical in nature and cannot be applied to individual consumers. They can be evaluated by the accuracy of their predictions but not by their modelling of the individual decisions which make up the whole. The latter may well be a serious shortcoming, since the key to obtaining a better understanding of aggregate behaviour may lie not in finding more complex empirical regularities but in incorporating those features of individual behaviour that observation shows us to be of importance.

Once the market area of a shopping centre has been derived it is then, in principle, possible to move over to the 'supply side' of the model and to investigate the behaviour of the retailers themselves with respect to locational decisions. For a fixed set of consumers an equilibrium distribution of retailers can be derived. The best-known versions of such equilibrium structures are those derived from Christaller's (1966) 'central place' theory. This theory, although designed to explain the existence of hierarchical structures of neighbouring towns and cities, can equally well be used to explain why there are hierarchical structures of shopping centres within towns. A typical hierarchical structure would have one large shopping centre (town) supplying all goods and services, some 'lower' order smaller centres supplying just a sub-group of the goods and services, and then even more smaller centres supplying a sub-group of this sub-group of the goods and services, etc. The two features which characterize a hierarchy are:

 (i) the wider the range of goods, the fewer the centres there are which provide them;
(ii) every larger centre provides all the goods and services provided by any smaller centre, as well as certain extra items.

The existence of approximately hierarchical structures is widely recognized and has been generally accepted as a 'stylized fact' which must be explained by any successful location model. Most of the emphasis on explaining how such hierarchical structures would come about has concentrated on the supply side (i.e. on the decisions of the entrepreneurs providing the goods), but in order to complete the model some assumptions about consumer behaviour have been needed and it is here that the theory has been least acceptable. In the full version of Christaller's model it is assumed that each consumer buys each good at the nearest source of supply for that good (the 'nearest centre' hypothesis). This is often justified by the prior behavioural assumption that on any given shopping trip any consumer will buy just one good (i.e. he visits just one shop)—the 'single-purpose shopping trip' hypothesis. In general these two assumptions are not equivalent but, if consumers are evenly spread throughout a town, have identical preferences and resources, and do buy each good separately, then in the long run all consumers will also finish up buying each good at the nearest source of supply (potential price differences would be competed away and the only factor distinguishing sources of supply would be their distance from the home). It is evident that neither assumption is, in practice, at all satisfactory. Consumers frequently (but not always) buy from more than one type of shop on a given shopping trip, and often do not buy a given good at the nearest source of supply. There is, indeed, evidence on whether the shops used by consumers are the the nearest source of supply for a particular good. Shepherd and Thomas (1980) in their survey of urban consumer behaviour say (p. 21):

Interest currently centres on the . . . concept which gives rise to the nearest centre hypothesis as the basic behavioural tenet of central place theory, i.e. that a consumer will visit the nearest centre supplying a good or service. However, it is now apparent that this inference results in a serious over-statement of behavioural realities. A considerable amount of information now exists which demonstrates the limitations of the hypothesis in the Western urban content . . . so that at best it can be considered only a partial explanation for consumer shopping behaviour. For example, Clark's . . . study of Christchurch shoppers indicated that only 50-60 per cent of convenience shopping trips could be predicted by the nearest centre hypothesis.

Hence it is generally agreed that although 'central place'-type models capture an important aspect of actual locational structure, they depend on assumptions about consumer behaviour which are highly unsatisfactory. Consumer behaviour, in the case where there is more than one good to be purchased, may well exhibit much more complex patterns than the nearest centre hypothesis would allow. Christaller himself discusses a situation in which the need to buy two separate goods leads the consumer to economize on trips by making a single trip to the nearest centre supplying both requirements. This 'multi-purpose' trip can occur even if *one* of the goods were supplied at a nearer centre. Thus Christaller showed that the existence of the possibility of multi-purpose trips would mean that the nearest centre hypothesis would have to be abandoned. However, in his formal model the analytical convenience of the nearest centre/single-purpose trip hypothesis was essential in enabling him to solve what was already a complex problem. Hence it follows that, before the equilibrium location of shops can be derived for a more satisfactory set of assumptions it will be necessary to analyse the individual consumer in the 'many good' case where multi-purpose trips are allowed. Virtually no work has been done on the problem of optimal consumer behaviour with respect to locational choice in the many-good case, and some authors have concluded that it is an intractable problem. Shepherd and Thomas say (p. 21):

. . . [S]hoppers may attempt to minimise total travel effort, often by combining shopping in a multi-purpose trip, rather than merely minimising the travel cost for an individual good. Thus a consumer may obtain both . . . goods at a high order centre which is more distant than the closer low order centre. Secondly, a shopper may travel to a distant centre if sales price savings exceed additional transport costs. It is difficult to envisage how such behavioural variations could be comprehensively incorporated into a modified central place theory.

However, the problem is not merely to construct a theory of consumer behaviour that permits discussion of several goods and predicts multi-purpose trips; it must also be consistent with the existence of a hierarchical set of shopping centres. A theory which predicted only one type of shopping trip on which all goods were bought (at the nearest centre selling all goods) would provide a reason for agglomeration (different types of shops locating together) but would not be able to explain the various degrees of agglomeration seen in hierarchical structures—no groups of shops providing less than the full range of goods could theoretically survive in such a model, since they would attract no custom. Thus a second requirement of any model which seeks to be consistent with central place theory is that, as well as predicting the existence of some multi-purpose trips for some consumers, it must predict that for some consumers trips are made on which not all goods are bought and which could therefore be made to the lowest-order centres, thus permitting a hierarchical structure of shopping centres to survive. In order to make the problem more concrete let us consider a town with just two centres (A and B) and where there are just two goods (1 and 2). The higher-order centre A sells both while the lower-order centre B sells only good 1. Under the nearest centre hypothesis consumers would visit centre B to buy good 1 only if they live nearer to B than to A. We recognize that even for these consumers the trips to centre A to buy good 2 would give rise to the possibility of saving the transport costs of a trip to B if both goods were purchased on the same occasion. The allowance of such multi-purpose trips (once the insistence on the nearest centre hypothesis is relaxed) provides a strong force encouraging the agglomeration of different types of shop and is in keeping with the observation that some trips are multi-purpose and that not all trips are to the nearest source of supply. However, once we recognize that every consumer has a motive for making multi-purpose trips we must, equally, be able to find a reason why at least some consumers also make single-purpose trips to the lower order centre. In our example we need to explain why some consumers, although buying both goods when they travel to A will sometimes buy good 1 also at centre B. If this pattern is to be explained it is evident that *the frequencies of purchasing the two goods must be different.* This hypothesis of differential frequency of purchasing, first put forward by Bacon (1971), is a key step in constructing a model of agglomeration and hierarchical structure, as Eaton and Lipsey (1982) have shown.

The argument roughly outlined here has shown how a model, in which the frequencies of purchases of the various goods are different, could produce consumer behaviour that is consistent with the existence of hierarchical structures of shopping centres and of multi-purpose trips and non-nearest centre shopping. However, this observation, although helpful itself, merely drives the argument back one stage further. There are two related questions that need to be answered:

 (i) Under what circumstances would a consumer prefer multi-purpose trips to separate single-purpose trips (even in the one-centre case)?
(ii) Why should frequencies be different? Why don't consumers adjust bundle sizes (the amount purchased per trip) so that, for example, all of good 1 is purchased on the multi-purpose trip on which good 2 is purchased at centre A?

The programme that we have outlined is, then, very ambitious. We need to be able to model both the frequency and location of a typical consumer's purchases in the many-good case for a given hierarchy of shopping centres. Only when this has been achieved can we hope to determine the market areas of the various centres and shops. Given the determination of market areas it would then be desirable to switch to the supply side and determine the equilibrium configuration of centres for our model. However, as Eaton and Lipsey (1982), writing of Bacon's problem in which the consumer, given the location of shops, optimizes the shopping plan, say (p. 60): 'If Bacon's problem defied general analytical

solution the firm-location does so doubly since to choose its optimal location every firm must solve each customer's problem for
each possible location and then aggregate these solutions to determine its demand as a function of its location.'

This book offers solutions to the first two parts of the problem—
that of the consumer optimum and that of the total demand (market
area)—for a given pattern of shops, but touches only briefly on the
integration with the supply side which would allow a unified and
improved 'central place'-type theory to be established. Even when
we concentrate purely on the demand side of the model we find that
there are three areas to be investigated which have received virtually
no attention in the literature. In order of logical structure it would
be natural to start within the determinants of frequency, in order to
show why frequencies of purchasing different goods need not be
the same. Having established this, the analysis could turn to the
consumer's choice of location when frequencies can differ, and
finally, the individual analysis could be integrated to show how
market areas can be determined in the many-good case. However,
the analysis of the simultaneous choice of frequency and location is
peculiarly awkward. As we shall see, the choice between locations is
essentially discrete in nature. For given frequencies of purchasing
we can make either a trip to A or one to B, but not one-half to each.
A trip is in certain aspects *fixed* and this fixed element cannot be
continuously varied as needed in order to use methods of classical
optimization. Frequency of shopping is in essence continuously
variable and so its optimization can be handled by conventional
techniques. The joint choice over frequency and location is then
very complicated and it is desirable to study choice over location
separately before combining these two new themes. Similarly, the
analysis of market areas in the many-good case, where frequency
and location are choice variables, is a formidable problem and so
we introduce the technique for its analysis by using it in the case
where location is variable but frequency is fixed. Hence the techniques are introduced in the simplest possible fashion before they
are integrated to produce the fully rounded model.

Chapters 2 and 3 discuss models of the determinants of the frequency of shopping in the single-centre case, first for the one-good
case and then for the two- or many-good cases. Chapter 2 investi-
gates a wide range of ideas that have been put forward to explain
the frequency of purchase of a single good. Only the simplest of

these are pursued in Chapter 3 for the two-good case because, as we shall see, the analysis greatly increases in complexity. However, certain ideas from the one-good case are suggestive for more refined work in the many-good case. A critical aim of this part of the book is to demonstrate the *possibility* that an optimal shopping programme *even in the single-centre case* could be made up of some multi-purpose trips and some single-purpose trips. As we have already argued, it is highly desirable to be able to produce a model which generates differential frequencies of shopping in order to be able to explain why hierarchies of centres emerge. If our explanation of differential frequencies depended on the existence of the hierarchy in the first place, then we should be faced with a 'chicken and egg' situation. Of course, as the hierarchy emerges, frequencies may tend to separate further but it is important to be able to show that, even were the hierarchy not to exist, there will be some separation of frequencies which may be sufficiently pronounced to encourage the emergence of the hierarchical structure.

Once a model has been developed which generates differential frequencies in a single-centre case, the analysis then takes the frequencies as fixed for a given consumer and shows, in Chapter 4, how the optimal choice of shopping locations will be made in the many-centre many-good case. There are a series of increasingly complex cases to consider even for this 'fixed frequency' model. The first case distinguishes centres purely by distance to the consumer and can be effectly reduced to the one-good case studied by many economists (such as Fetter (1924), Hotelling (1929), and others). In such a case, quantity (bundle size) may be variable, as in the work of Hoover (1937), because of price elasticity of demand. The second case fixes quantities and frequencies but allows centres to differ in the range of goods provided. This case was analysed by Bacon (1971) under the assumption that there is no price competition (i.e. a given good is the same price at all centres selling that good). This second case can be generalized to allow for price differences between centres.

Chapter 5 develops techniques for determining the market areas of the different centres when frequencies are fixed and identical for all consumers. The analysis for the single-good case is well known in this fixed frequency case but virtually no consideration appears to have been given to the many-good case and, accordingly, substantial attention is paid to its treatment. An important consideration is that the technique of analysis used (parametric programming) can be adapted to the more complex situations that arise when both frequency and location are choice variables.

Once models for these three aspects have been developed it is possible to make a synthesis in Chapter 6. This shows firstly how a consumer simultaneously chooses frequency and location in a multi-centre multi-good model and then discusses how market areas can be identified in such a case. Emphasis is placed on showing how mixed frequency shopping programmes emerge and how some consumers use both higher- and lower-order centres for some goods. This analysis produces purchases which are not necessarily made at the nearest centre, as well as multi-purpose trips. This shows that the model developed can produce certain key features of consumer behaviour which are not only more satisfactory than those utilized in traditional central place theory, but which are also likely to be consistent with the patterns of shopping centres predicted by central place theory. In particular, not only are the predictions of the model likely to be consistent with the existence of a hierarchical structure of shopping centres, but they are also likely to reinforce tendencies towards hierarchy which exist on the supply side.

So far the analysis, particularly in discussing market areas, assumes that all consumers are identical, except with respect to the distances to the various shopping centres. Of course households differ in many ways, but most of these are only incidentally connected with their spatial behaviour. One important aspect in which they can differ and which is directly related to their spatial behaviour is that of the nature of the transport opportunities open to them. Not only car ownership, but also the existence or not of bus routes will affect the choice of centre. Clearly, as well as frequency and location, the consumer can often choose the mode of travel to the shops, and indeed this may interact with the other two variables. The type of model presented in this book permits a deterministic model of modal choice. Since virtually all other work on this important subject is either aggregative or probabilistic in nature it is of considerable interest to sketch in Chapter 7 how modal choice can be analysed in multi-centre, multi-activity models. There are indeed some important insights to be gained here. We can hope to show why consumers living next to a shopping centre will walk to it while those living further away use the bus or their car (even though the consumers are alike in all respects other than distance). At the same time, we discuss the reasons why a given consumer may use different modes to visit different centres and may even use different modes to visit the same centre on different trips.

Chapter 8 performs two functions. First, it reviews the model and ideas used and attempts to summarize and evaluate them and second, it looks forward, in the sense of sketching how the central core of the arguments might be used to generate further insights into spatial matters. First, an integrated supply/demand model (of the 'central place theory' type) is discussed. Next, the role of family structure on shopping patterns is sketched. Both approaches then lead to considerations of disequilibrium in the model, either purely because of lags in entry and exit or because of the inevitably changing nature of consumer demand. Changes in household structure (which may affect particular neighbourhoods), such as the changing demographic structure of new housing estates or general changes (say) in transport costs, will tend to alter the equilibrium distribution of shops. Hence studies of historical shifts in the patterns of shops can be related to changing consumer circumstances. A further aspect of the model which is discussed is its relation to urban planning. Not only do the ideas have relevance to the planned provision of shopping centres but also to the provision of public transport facilities and of non-shopping activities. The existence of bus routes or of car parks clearly affects shopping patterns and these features can be integrated into models of the type shown here. Also, the existence of a non-shopping activity, for example a public library, can induce 'joint-purpose' trips and hence alter shopping patterns. Again, the model is shown to be able to incorporate such ideas.

Before we start the analysis it may also be helpful to say something on methodology and technique. Much of the analysis uses mathematical models but since both economists and spatial geographers are familiar in general with a mathematical approach to their subjects I have not felt it necessary, nor would have been able, to dispense with these techniques. However, one particular technique used, that of parametric programming, may not be so familiar and I have taken more time to develop its use. Certain central aspects of the book, notably the choice of frequency in the many-good case (with one or many centres), would require a mixed non-linear/integer programme and its associated parametric version to obtain general solutions. Such solutions would not be analytic in the sense that they could be written down in a closed form. Rather they would be algorithmic in nature—a set of rules might be derived which would show how to find the optimum in a *finite* number of steps whatever the exact values of the constants of the problem. However, there is no doubt that the algorithms would be very complex and would have to be specially developed. The book would then start to be dominated by the need to provide general proofs. Accordingly, it has been decided to present general cases only where these are easily accessible. In more difficult instances only the two-variable case is thoroughly analysed. This is usually sufficient to show whether or not differential frequency and hierarchy will be consistent with the approach taken. Generalizations to three or more goods may be possible, but it appears that the fundamental insights come from the extension from one to two goods. Even in the two-good case it rapidly becomes clear that the analysis is very difficult once choice over frequency is involved. This is because there is a discrete shift in the cost function depending on whether or not two goods are purchased on the same trip. This difficulty, which leads to the need to develop an algorithm to solve the general two-good case, also has the important effect of limiting the generality of consumer behaviour considered. Rather than maximizing utility subject to an income constraint, it is found very much easier to minimize total costs subject to expenditure requirements for each good. The lack of substitutability that this implies is clearly a shortcoming of the model presented. However, it does seem that were the model to be generalized to incorporate a utility function this would not have the effect of *automatically* equalizing frequencies and hence of being inconsistent with hierarchical structures of shopping centres. Indeed it seems possible, depending on the relative strengths of the preferences for the two goods, that frequencies could converge or diverge to any extent. Thus the spirit of the analysis appears unaffected by this strong simplification.

Because the models cannot be solved by analytical means it is not immediately possible to say that there will always be (or not be) differential frequency shopping programmes and hence that there will always be hierarchical structures of shopping centres. What is the central concern of this book is to demonstrate the *possibility* that such shopping patterns can exist and to indicate also that their existence (when it occurs) is not always going to be over such a small set of consumers that hierarchical structures could never be sustained. It is important to be able to show not only that they are likely to exist under a fairly wide range of situations, but also that under other situations no hierarchy within the town will exist. Many small towns in Europe have only one shopping centre and it is obvious that the total size of the town is crucially related to the possibility of the emergence of lower-order centres. With these facts in mind it will be appreciated that the analysis must attack the problem of whether a hierarchy might exist, and not whether it must exist.

A final limitation of the model should be noted. In choosing between centres, consumers are affected not only by the purely spatial differences between centres (distance and availability of shops) but also by the style of the shop, the quality of service available, and a whole host of other factors. These variables, which are much emphasized in the marketing literature, for example Engel, Kollat, and Blackwell (1973), are merely put aside for the present. No doubt they could be incorporated into a formal model of the type developed in this book, but that in itself would be a major undertaking and would add perhaps rather little to our understanding of how the spatial nature of the provision of shops affects consumer behaviour and is in turn affected by consumer behaviour.

2

OPTIMAL FREQUENCY AND BUNDLE SIZE IN THE SINGLE-GOOD SINGLE-CENTRE CASE

The introduction has already made the point, central to this book, that in order to study spatial behaviour of consumers we must be able to model the frequency of their shopping. Because the act of travelling to a centre takes time, and because time is costly to the consumer in some way or another, there is a critical link between space and time for the consumer. It is this link which, we aim to show, can produce a spectrum of frequencies of purchases for the various goods bought by the household. If frequencies are different then it is possible for a hierarchy of shopping centres to exist, but if frequencies are all equal and if multi-purpose shopping trips are allowed then all shopping will be done at the nearest centre supplying the whole range of goods. In such a case, no lower-order centre (supplying just a subset of goods) could survive since it would do no trade, and so although there would be strong incentives for agglomeration of shops, there would be no hierarchical structure. Clearly, differential frequency is the key fact to be explained. However, very little formal work has been done on the determinants of frequency even in the one-good case, and that work which has been done is very scattered in the literature. At the same time there are a large number of factors which it has been suggested can affect frequency, and it is easiest to review these in the simpler, single-good model. Accordingly, this chapter reviews a wide range of ideas on the determinants of the frequency of purchasing a single good, while the next chapter concentrates on a special case in order to carry out the much more difficult analysis of the choice of frequency in the two-good case. At the same time we will obtain values for the 'bundle' size (i.e. the amount of shopping purchased per trip).

It is obvious from casual introspection that the frequencies of purchases of different goods do vary, but there is little systematic evidence on this and there is virtually no empirical work published on the determinants of the frequency of shopping. Johnson and Hensher (1979) estimate a model of the determinants of shopping frequency (for goods overall) as between households, but give little discussion of the role of the variables used to explain frequency. Bacon (1968) gives some limited evidence suggesting that different goods are purchased at different frequencies (and different shopping centres visited at different frequencies), but there is no published evidence of the form required on the differential frequencies of individual households. However, an important finding in Bacon's study (admittedly now considerably out of date) was that a very large number of people regularly shopped several times a week for the same category of goods. This observation suggests, as we shall see, that the simple model, taken as the starting point for the analysis later in the book, is perhaps best thought of as a good first approximation rather than as an essentially complete characterization of the determinants of the frequency of shopping.

We can begin our investigation of the one-good case with the observation that most economic models which have analysed spatial purchasing behaviour have discussed the models as if there were one single trip made per unit time period. The work of Hotelling takes the quantity purchased on this trip as fixed, while some followers of Hotelling, for example Hoover (1937), Smithies (1941), and Ackley (1941), have argued that the amount purchased is price elastic and should be modelled following a conventional demand function derived from consumption theory. A similar tendency is evident in the work on central place theory. Both schools implicitly assume that the frequency is the same for all consumers. There is an obvious flaw in such an approach—it says nothing about the time dimension of purchasing behaviour. All these models imply that, whether we are discussing the consumer's income measured over a week or over a year, the consumer will spend all of that on *one* trip to the preferred shopping centre. Moreover, frequency in such models is clearly invariant with respect to changes in any parameters (incomes, prices, or transport costs) within the period under study. Not only is such an approach implausible (consumers do not shop once a month even if their income is received monthly), but it has effects on the whole of the spatial equilibrium model. If consumers further away from a centre can offset high transport costs by less frequent shopping then the range of a centre may well be different from that predicted in the fixed frequency case.

Clearly, there is a relationship betwen consumption behaviour and purchasing behaviour, since the latter is the means by which the former is made possible, but they are not identical. Consumption behaviour usually deals with the problem of the time dimension either by ignoring it or else by assuming that it takes place at a continuous and constant rate. Purchasing behaviour, obviously, is not a continuous phenomenon but is carried out at discrete intervals. This observation alerts us to the fact that inventories of goods are an everyday feature of household behaviour and play the linking role between purchasing and consumption. With this in mind, we can identify at least one reason why consumers do not shop once a year or even once a month. The amount of inventory would have to be very large (a whole month's or year's consumption). This would be expensive both in terms of money tied up and in terms of storage space. At the same time, the inconvenience of bringing home a whole month's shopping on a single trip would be very great. These forces would tend to limit the size of bundle and inventory the household would wish to carry. However, once we postulate a force which tends to raise costs as inventories grow and frequency decreases, it is necessary to identify a counterbalancing cost which will ensure that the consumer does not shop as often as physically possible (thus reducing inventory costs to a minimum because of the small bundle size). The most obvious cost which increases with frequency of shopping is the time and money cost of travelling to the shopping centre and visiting the various shops in the centre.

All of the models we present will have these two opposing forces, and the optimum frequency is determined by their interaction. There are a series of models which have been suggested in the literature and we take many ideas from them. There is one dichotomy of particular importance in these models which we should stress from the outset. The simpler models take the total purchased per time period (rather than per trip) as fixed. The problem is then to find the combination of frequency and bundle size which satisfies this constraint and which minimizes the cost of purchasing. The second approach is a form of dual to the first. It defines a utility function over the amount per consumer per time period and has as its objective the choice of frequency and bundle size which maximizes utility subject to an income constraint. As we shall see, the former problem, since it does not explicitly involve an indirect utility function, is much simpler to handle.

(a) FIXED QUANTITY, FIXED ORDER COST MODEL

The simplest model of the frequency of shopping behaviour is that suggested by Reinhardt (1973) and based on classical inventory theory.

The given consumer faces a single shopping centre which sells the good at a fixed ('mill') price of p per unit. The consumer requires Q units of the good per period for consumption. The consumer purchases the good in bundles of size q (the 'lot' size) at a frequency of f per unit time. The interval between successive purchases (d) is therefore $1/f$. As well as the purchase cost of the good (pQ per unit time) the consumer incurs two other costs. Each trip to the shopping centre costs money and holding an inventory of the good also costs money. The assumptions that we make about these two costs will determine the nature of the optimum values for frequency and bundle sizes. The standard assumption made about the costs of trips to the centre (the so-called 'order' cost) is that these are strictly proportional to the number of trips to the centre and are independent of the amount ordered on any trip. Let us denote the cost of making one trip (placing one order) by t. The cost of running an inventory is proportional to the average amount in the inventory multiplied by the time span over which the inventory is run. We denote the cost of storing one money unit of the good for one time period as I. In order to finalize the model we need to make four further assumptions:

  (i) the good is purchased only when the inventory is empty;
 (ii) the consumer uses up the good at a steady rate;
(iii) the consumer never goes short of the good (purchases as soon as the inventory is empty);
(iv) all bundles purchased over time are of the same size.

Under these assumptions the graph of the inventory level against time can be represented as in Figure 2.1.

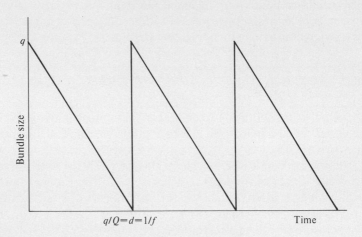

Fig. 2.1 Inventory levels for a single good over time

A model of this type is known as a 'lot size system' and is thoroughly analysed by Naddor (1966). The total cost per unit time is

$$TC = pqf + tf + cqp \qquad (2.1)$$

where $q =$ bundle size, $f =$ frequency, and $c = I/2$. This must be maximized subject to the fixed quantity restriction

$$Q = qf. \qquad (2.2)$$

Simple substitution of equation (2.2) into equation (2.1) plus differentiation yields the optimal values

$$f^* = \sqrt{(cQp/t)}, \qquad (2.3)$$

$$d^* = \sqrt{(t/cpQ)}, \qquad (2.4)$$

$$q^* = \sqrt{(tQ/cp)}. \qquad (2.5)$$

The final equation is very familiar in economics, being known as 'the square root rule', and has been used not only in industrial inventory theory but also in such studies as models of the optimal holding of cash for transactions. This simple model has a number of features which are of interest in the spatial content:

(i) As total consumption increases, frequency and bundle size both increase. It is particularly important to notice that frequency responds to Q since this plays the role of the exogenous income level in a conventional utility-maximizing framework.

(ii) Frequency rises with inventory costs while bundle size falls. The more expensive it is to have money tied up in an inventory the more frequently the consumer shops and the lower the value of the bundle size.

(iii) The higher the cost of transport (which is our order cost) the less frequently the consumer shops and the larger will be the bundle size. This result is of particular interest in the spatial content because even if consumers were alike in all other respects, they live at different distances from the shops and hence must face different transport costs. This implies that the frequency of shopping will differ systematically throughout the town. Furthermore, changes in transport costs relative to other costs will produce changes in frequency. Hence changes like those of the 1970s, when there were unprecedented shifts in transport costs, might predict substantial changes in the frequency of purchasing and hence of the size of market areas.

It is useful to look at this model in more detail before going on to other cases. There are three different money costs of running an inventory that are mentioned in the literature. They are:

(i) costs of running the inventory (heating, refrigeration, security);

(ii) opportunity costs of the interest foregone on the money spent on the goods held in the inventory;

(iii) costs due to perishability, which mean that the household has to buy more than it wished to consume in order to allow for wastage.

Reinhardt (1973) and Sharir (1978) give all three reasons for the existence of money costs of holding an inventory, while Lentenk, Harwitz, and Narula (1981) place special emphasis on the role of perishability.

Providing that all three costs are such as to be modelled by a cost term proportional to the *value* of the bundle size (which determines the average amount held in the inventory) then model (a) has already dealt with this phenomenon. However, there are certain aspects of the formulation which deserve closer attention in the context of household behaviour.

The costs of running the inventory are of negligible importance in the household and indeed can even be regarded as fixed costs. The refrigerator and freezer will be switched on however little they are used.

The cost of the money tied up in the inventory is substantial and clearly can be of a magnitude to have a large effect on the frequency of shopping in practice. However, let us consider the example of a household spending £100 every two weeks on the composite good. The effect of shopping once a week for bundles of £50 rather than once a fortnight for bundles of £100 is that over a fifty-week year (with an interest rate of 10 per cent) the household gains an extra £2.50 in interest from the more frequent shopping. If bus fares were 10p a trip then the extra twenty-five trips would just be worthwhile. Clearly, the financial inventory costs are likely to prevent once-a-year or even once-a-month shopping, but it seems unlikely that in this type of model they would be sufficiently important relative to transport costs to explain the very high frequency shopping patterns (two or three times a week) reported by Bacon (1968). Another factor is probably needed in order to explain the willingness of the consumer to make so many trips.

A further aspect of the model is that it assumes that if the household were to economize on the value of the inventory held, the extra money gained would be used to earn interest or to reduce borrowing costs. It is not necessary that the housewife (if she is the main shopper) is involved in borrowing or lending, but merely that the household is collectively involved in such activities and that there is a free transfer of money between the various agents in the household. We shall return to this point later, in model (e).

The costs due to perishability are no doubt important for certain classes of goods and will help to push up the total inventory costs of the household, but certainly cannot be taken on their own to be very important.

(a*) FIXED VALUE, FIXED ORDER COST MODEL

A variation on the basic model which is central to developments in later chapters is the case where the value (V) purchased per unit time rather than the quantity purchased per unit time is taken as constant.

We must now choose q (and f) so as to minimize equation (2.1) subject to the requirement that

$$V = pqf. \tag{2.2*}$$

The optimal frequency is now

$$f^* = \sqrt{(cV/t)} \tag{2.3*}$$

with duration between trips

$$d^* = \sqrt{(t/cV)} \tag{2.4*}$$

and optimal bundle size

$$q^* = \sqrt{(tV/cp^2)}. \tag{2.5*}$$

There is a great deal of similarity in structure between the two sets of solutions, but the role of price differs. In model (a) frequency increases with price and bundle size decreases, while in model (a*) frequency is invariant with respect to price but bundle size is a more rapidly decreasing function of price.

These two cases cannot be formally justified on the basis of any implicit theory of consumer behaviour, although it might be reasonable to argue that a family of given size has a certain physical requirement for a good which is invariant to any of the economic circumstances surrounding the purchase of the good. We next investigate for completeness a utility-maximizing approach to the choice of optimal frequency since such a model removes the arbitrariness of the constraints.

(b) UTILITY AS A FUNCTION OF QUANTITY, FIXED ORDER COST MODEL

We can now take the obvious economic generalization of model (a) and instead of fixing the total quantity to be purchased (and consumed) per time period we can fix income available per time period at Y. The consumer then attempts to maximize utility given the budget constraints imposed by the various costs. The model can be written:

maximize

$$U = U(qf) \tag{2.6}$$

subject to

$$Y = pqf + cpq + tf \tag{2.7}$$

where U stands for utility per time period.

We are assuming that Y is disposable income net of saving. This system can be optimized by standard Legrangean methods to yield

$$f^* = -c + \sqrt{(c^2 + cY/t)}, \tag{2.8}$$

$$q^* = \{-t + \sqrt{(t^2 + tY/c)}\}/p, \tag{2.9}$$

$$Q^* = \{Y - 2\sqrt{(c^2t^2 + ctY)}\}/p. \tag{2.10}$$

These results are clearly closely related to the fixed value model of equations (2.3*) and (2.5*), but there are some interesting features:

(i) The results are invariant with respect to the exact form of the utility function. This is inevitable in the single-good case—the costs are merely rearranged so as to permit the maximum quantity to be purchased per unit time which will be the utility-maximizing amount irrespective of the function.

(ii) Demand per unit time (or per trip) cannot be written as a function of the delivered price $(p + t)$ whatever the utility function. The spatial demand functions which relate quantity to delivered price must be derived from a different cost structure. If we use the same cost structure but take frequency as fixed at $\bar{f}$ (as in Hotelling-type models), the constrained maximization yields

$$q^* = (Y - t\bar{f})/(p\bar{f} + pc), \tag{2.11}$$

which confirms the point made earlier.

(iii) The optimum solution can be represented graphically as in Figure 2.2. We can see that the budget line is convex but cuts both axes, while the indifference curve is also convex but is asymptotic to both axes, thus yielding a tangency solution.

(iv) As with the fixed quantity model, we can see that when the storage cost tends to zero the frequency will decrease and the bundle size will increase. In this model it is clearly storage costs which prevent the consumer from shopping once a year. Transport costs have the opposite effect, since as they become small frequency rises and bundle size shrinks.

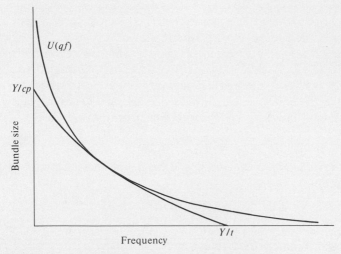

Fig. 2.2 Utility-maximizing frequency for a single good

(c) UTILITY MAXIMIZATION, ORDER COSTS PROPORTIONAL TO QUANTITY

So far we have followed Reinhardt in assuming that the transport cost element is proportional solely to the number of trips. However, we have seen that Hotelling and his followers used the much less plausible assumption that transport costs would be strictly proportional to the amount transported on a trip so that the bundle size affects transport costs. The model becomes:

maximize

$$U = U(qf)$$

subject to

$$Y = pqf + tqf + cpq. \tag{2.12}$$

The optimal values are a bundle size tending to zero (per unit of time) and frequency tending to infinity. This result is not surprising. The costs of transport can be held constant by increasing frequency and lowering bundle size while the latter allows storage costs to diminish. The unacceptability of the modelling of the transport cost element is shown by its consequences. In concrete terms, it assumes that the transport cost for shopping ten times for a one-pound bag of potatoes is the same as that of shopping once for a ten-pound bag. This cannot be taken even as a good approximation in the context of consumer behaviour.

There is a special case of this model which is relevant to the Hotelling-type models. If storage costs can be arranged to cost nothing (which is the implicit assumption in such models) then although the solutions for bundle size and frequency become indeterminate, the value of the optimum quantity is given by

$$Q^* = Y/(p+t). \qquad (2.13)$$

Further, if frequency is fixed at a value $\bar{f}$ then the optimum bundle size becomes

$$q^* = Y/(p+t)\bar{f}. \qquad (2.14)$$

Hence we can see that the case where demand per trip is a function of the delivered price requires that:

  (i) transport costs are porportional to quantity and frequency;
 (ii) frequency is exogenously fixed;
(iii) storage costs are zero.

The demand function used in location theory (demand is proportional to delivered price) would have to be of a very limited functional form, and relies upon a series of rather implausible assumptions.

(d) FIXED QUANTITY, FIXED TRANSPORT COSTS, INVENTORY WITH LIMITED-SPACE MODEL

We turn next to an investigation of the role of the inventory in the determination of frequency. So far we have assumed without discussion that the inventory imposes a money cost on the consumer. There are in fact many ways in which an inventory can limit the bundle size and we begin with the simple idea that there may be a limit to the physical amount of goods that can be stored. Such an argument, which is obviously plausible for certain industrial goods, may also be true for some consumption goods. In particular, the size of the refrigerator or deep-freezer will limit the amount of perishables that can be stored. We can assume that in general this is unlikely to be an important factor for the average good. The modelling and analysis of limited storage room is quite straight-forward. We need to minimize total costs subject to the bundle size fitting into the limited inventory:

minimize

$$TC = pqf + tf + cpq$$

subject to

$$q \leq S, \; qf = Q \qquad (2.15)$$

where S is the amount of storage space in physical units. The technique is to consider the unconstrained solution:

$$q^* = \sqrt{(tQ/cp)}$$

and compare this with the value of S. If q^* is less than S then the size limit of the inventory is unimportant since the consumer would not wish to use it all. If q^* is greater than S then the inventory size matters since the consumer wishes to hold more. In such a case the maximum bundle size is determined by the inventory and the frequency reflects this:

$$q^* = S, \; f^* = Q/S. \qquad (2.16)$$

Over time the acquisition of more storage space would lead to a relaxation of the constraint for a household and a decrease in frequency.

(e) FIXED QUANTITY, FIXED TRANSPORT COSTS WITH FINANCIAL CONSTRAINTS MODEL

An important feature of household behaviour which could affect the frequency of shopping is the internal financial arrangement. In many cases the husband is the sole earner and he gives a periodic allowance (weekly or monthly) to the wife, who is responsible for the shopping. The wife has no access to other funds and thus cannot spend more per payment period than this allowance. This arrangement would impose a very strong constraint on the frequency of shopping when the payment period is short. With a weekly allowance the wife cannot shop once a fortnight because there is no way of obtaining the money for the extra week's worth of shopping. If such constraints are thought to be the most likely reason why shopping is not infrequent then we would still be left to explain the phenomenon of housewives who shop more than once a week. Furthermore, these housewives clearly hold cash (or have a current bank account) and will be in surplus during the week but will not be earning interest from this money. There is a general problem in these models as to why people shop so often. With any fixed elements in transport costs this is an expensive procedure, yet it does not seem that housewives or families make strenuous efforts to offset these costs by increasing interest receipts (or decreasing borrowing). It does appear that some further force is at work in many cases. One such factor is clearly related to the uncertainty facing the family. It is not possible to plan out the exact pattern of consumption for (say) a week in advance, and so the shopper must be prepared to make occasional trips for items which have been unforeseen. This will also require the holding of precautionary cash where the opportunity cost of interest gain must be weighed against the disutility of incurring a shortage and going without something. Such considerations will certainly lead to more frequent shopping behaviour than in the model with certainty, but these extra trips are likely to be much smaller in terms of bundle size. Many neighbourhood shops may gain a good deal of business from such unanticipated shopping.

(f) UTILITY AS A FUNCTION OF GOODS AND LEISURE TIME, FIXED TRANSPORT COSTS MODEL

Since the work of Becker (1965) and De Serpa (1971) it has been recognized that the actual time spent undertaking certain activities can affect the household's optimal choice. This happens through a twofold effect, since time-intensive activities mean that less time is available for earning income and for enjoying leisure activities (which make a direct contribution to the level of utility of the household). In the context of shopping behaviour, Reinhardt (1973), Sharir (1978), and Lentenk, Harwitz, and Narula (1981) have all investigated the effect of the time spent shopping on the optimal frequency.

Reinhardt takes the simplest view that each *trip* to a centre takes a certain amount of time (independent of the amount of goods purchased) and that the actual purchase of a good also takes a given amount of time (which is independent of the bundle size). Each unit of time spent shopping is assumed to involve a money cost (the implicit value of the shopper's time) so that model (a) needs to be modified by the addition of an extra term to the expression for costs:

$$TC = pQ + tf + cpq + wbf \qquad (2.17)$$

where w = value of 1 unit of shoppers time and b = total time taken to travel to centre and to buy the good. This can obviously be re-written in the form

$$TC = pQ + t^*f + cpq \qquad (2.18)$$

where

$$t^* = t + wb \qquad (2.19)$$

which has as its optimal value

$$f^* = \sqrt{(cpQ/t^*)}. \qquad (2.20)$$

As the value of time taken to shop increases the frequency of shopping will clearly decrease. However, the formulation of this model is not altogether satisfactory since the value put on time is only an implicit cost and not a direct cost. It would clearly be preferable to construct a model in which the effects of time are modelled directly. This is the approach of Sharir and of Lentenk *et al.* The first step is to define a utility function which has both the level of goods consumed and the amount of leisure enjoyed per period as arguments:

$$U = U(Q, L) \qquad (2.21)$$

where L = number of hours leisure per period. The amount of time taken over shopping (S) per period is given by

$$S = fb \qquad (2.22)$$

and the total time constraint is then

$$L = T - H - S \qquad (2.23)$$

where H = number of hours working per period and T = total number of hours available per period. The income constraint is even more general than before in that it allows income to be endogenous rather than exogenous:

$$wH = pqf + cpq + tf \qquad (2.24)$$

where w = wage per hour. It can be seen that time enters the budget constraint through its effect on total earnings. There is no solution to this model which is valid whatever the utility function, but there is a useful relation between two of the optimal values which is invariant with respect to the form of the function:

$$q^* = f^* (wb + t)/cp. \qquad (2.25)$$

If we take a specific form for the utility function then we can obtain explicit solutions. The simplest form is the so-called 'Bergson' function (see Barten (1977) for a survey of functional forms commonly used in demand analysis):

$$U = (qf)^\alpha L \qquad (2.26)$$

where $\alpha > 0$. The optimal values of equation (2.26) subject to equations (2.22), (2.23), and (2.24) are

$$f^* = [-c(1 + 2\alpha) + \sqrt{\{c^2 (1 + 2\alpha)^2 + 4c\alpha Tw (1 + \alpha)/t^*\}}]$$
$$/2(1 + \alpha) \qquad (2.27)$$

and

$$q^* = [-t^* (1 + 2\alpha) + \sqrt{\{t^{*2} (1 + 2\alpha)^2 + 4 t^*\alpha Tw (1 + \alpha)/c\}}]$$
$$/2 p(1 + \alpha) \qquad (2.28)$$

where $t^* = wb + t$. L (or H) is also determined in this fashion. The basic structure of these equations is very similar to equations (2.8) and (2.9). The qualitative effects of changes in parameters on the variables are shown in Table 2.1.

For this special case the results are exactly as expected. Factors which lead to an ability to purchase more goods (W and T) tend to increase both frequency and bundle size, while price affects only

TABLE 2.1

Qualitative effects on parameter shifts in model (f)

	Parameter	f^*	q^*
α	Preference for goods	+	+
c	Inventory costs	+	−
T	Total time available	+	+
w	Wage rate	+	+
p	Price of goods	0	−
b	Time for a shopping trip	−	+
t	Cost of travel	−	+

bundle size. Inventory costs and costs of travel have the same effect as in other models. The new variable (time taken over shopping) acts in exactly the same fashion as the cost of travel, and indeed we see that in the case of the Bergson function we can construct a total cost of shopping variable, t^*. This makes more acceptable the practice of using the implicit costs of travel in the fixed quantity models such as the one set up by Reinhardt. As expected, making allowance for the cost of shopping time implicit in the wage foregone tends to reduce frequency. This factor may be important in cases where less time spent over shopping can genuinely lead to a rise in income. Of course in households where one person does the shopping and the other works there is no simple link. An hour less shopping per week by the housewife does not mean that the husband is automatically released to do one more hour's work. However, if the household arranges matters so that the two partners do have some activities done by either then the release of one hour from shopping can affect the time spent working through a redivision of this common activity.

(g) UTILITY RELATED TO GOODS AND THE INCONVENIENCE OF SHOPPING, FIXED TRANSPORT COSTS MODEL

We are still looking for a factor which will tend to avoid infrequent trips with large bundle sizes, since all our previous analysis has suggested that weighing the total costs (direct plus indirect) of extra shopping trips against inventory costs would tend to lead to people shopping more infrequently than is often observed. One factor that we have so far ignored is the actual inconvenience or difficulty of transporting large amounts of shopping from the centre to home. Unless a car is being used this is clearly an important consideration. The simple physical effort of handling a complete week's shopping on one trip when travelling by bus or bicycle, or when walking, does give a very plausible reason for why shoppers should wish to carry smaller bundles and hence to shop more frequently. Even the use of a car cannot avoid this problem altogether if the car park is not situated next to the shops. This suggests that, depending on the mode of transport available, the behaviour of individuals may be very different, and we shall return to this issue in Chapter 7.

The problem with this idea is that of how to model the way in which inconvenience should enter the utility function. We can postulate the following effects:

(i) the larger the physical amount of shopping carried on a trip the lower will be the total utility per period *ceteris paribus*;
(ii) the more trips that are carried out the greater the inconvenience and the lower the level of utility from this case;
(iii) the longer the distance to be transported the lower the level of utility;
(iv) the more carrying-intensive is the mode used the lower will be the utility (for example walking is worse than cycling).

The main thrust of the argument is that because of the associated inconvenience increasing bundle size will eventually act as a brake on the tendency to shop infrequently, and that the trade-off between these two arguments may be different from their trade-off as regards total quantity purchased per period of time (which is the first argument of the utility function). A simple form of utility function that would serve our purpose could be

$$U = U(qf, dbq^\beta f) \qquad (2.29)$$

where d = distance to be carried, m = mode parameter, and where the first argument of the function relates to the amount of goods consumed per unit of time and the second to the degree of inconvenience experienced in shopping per unit of time. Of course the second argument is a 'bad' so that in general terms we have

$$U = U(Q,N) \qquad (2.30)$$

where N = level of inconvenience, with

$$dU/dQ > 0, \ dU/dN < 0. \qquad (2.31)$$

In the specific form of equation (2.29) the parameter β measures the extent to which quantity per trip contributes towards inconvenience. If β is greater than unity then inconvenience will increase faster than the bundle size. The parameters d and m will not affect behaviour in our model with a consumer facing a single centre at a given distance and having just one mode of transport available. However, once we discuss choice between centres in Chapter 6 and choice between transport modes in Chapter 7 they could have an important role.

In order to obtain some simple results we need to assume a specific

form for the function (2.29), and we again use a Bergson form:
$$U = (qf)(q^\beta f)^{-\alpha}. \tag{2.32}$$

There are some important restrictions on the parameter values required to keep the function economically interesting. In order for the level of inconvenience to be a bad we have the restriction that α is positive. Secondly, in order that larger bundles (at the same frequency) and higher frequencies (as the same bundle size) both lead to increasing utility we require that α is less than unity and $\beta\alpha$ is less than unity. We rewrite the utility function in the form

$$U = (q)^{1-\beta\alpha}(f)^{1-\alpha} \tag{2.33}$$

and using the monotone transform of taking equation (2.33) to the power $(1/(1-\alpha)$ we arrive at the form

$$U = q^\gamma f \tag{2.34}$$

where

$$\gamma = (1 - \beta\alpha)/(1 - \alpha). \tag{2.35}$$

We can now maximize equation (2.35) subject to the simple budget constraint

$$Y = pqf + cpq + tf$$

to obtain
$$f^* = [- Y(\gamma - 1) - ct\,(1 + \gamma) + \sqrt{\{[Y(\gamma - 1) + ct\,(1 + \gamma)]^2}} \\ + 4cYt\}]/2t. \tag{2.36}$$

This result must be compared with equation (2.8) to reveal the extra effects of introducing an inconvenience factor into the utility function (everything else remaining the same):

$$f^* = -c + \sqrt{(c^2 + cY/t)}. \tag{2.8}$$

It can be seen that at a value of $\gamma = 1$ equation (2.36) collapses back to equation (2.8) and this is consistent with the fact that for γ to equal unity the parameter α must be zero, and inconvenience is then not a function of bundle size or frequency. As α increases the importance of inconvenience increases and we see that γ will increase if β is less than unity and decrease if β is greater than unity. Equation (2.36) shows us that as γ increases the optimal frequency decreases (and vice versa). Hence we see that as the importance of inconvenience increases the frequency of shopping will increase if β is greater than unity. The other parameters have similar effects to the previous model.

This special case is of considerable interest since it not only shows how to introduce the idea of inconvenience into the utility function but also shows that if the consumer is more affected by the heaviness of the bundle than by the number of trips on which the bundle has to be carried ($\beta > 1$) the consumer will make more trips than would be predicted by a model on which his sole interest in raising frequency was to lower inventory costs. Having established that such a result is possible, and noting that for small γ the difference between equations (2.36) and (2.8) could be substantial, it is not necessary to consider the general case. We have established what we need to know, namely that it is possible for inconvenience of shopping to have a substantial effect on frequency.

(h) PRICE DISCOUNTS FOR BULK PURCHASES

So far we have assumed that the price paid per unit of the good in the shop is constant irrespective of the number of units purchased. Both Reinhardt and Sharir relax this assumption by arguing that as the quantity purchased increased the per unit price would decrease. It is certainly true that, even at a given shop, larger packets are often cheaper per unit than small packets for items which are sold packaged in various sizes, but it is rather difficult to assess how much of the total range of shopping this phenomenon will apply to. We have already argued in Chapter 2 that price differentials are important, but as between centres rather than for different bundle sizes. Clearly, if there are price differentials then consumers will be pushed towards buying larger bundles and frequency would drop both in the fixed quantity cost-minimizing model and in the utility-maximizing model. This idea is perhaps more important in the many-good model where different goods are subject to different rates of discount for bulk purchase.

CONCLUSION

We have seen that a great many factors can be introduced into the modelling of the determinants of the choice of frequency of shopping in the case of a single good. In all models the crucial elements appear to be on the one hand order related cost elements (transport and time costs) which tend to decrease frequency and increase bundle size, and on the other hand inventory-related costs which tend to reduce bundle size and increase frequency.

It is possible to start from general utility-maximizing models where utility is not only a function of the amount purchased per period or of the leisure time left after the shopping has been done, but also a negative function of the ease of shopping. However, all these attempts to generalize results, although they increase the realism of the modelling of the situation facing the consumer, exact a heavy price in terms of the complexity of the results. Indeed, only the simplest lot size models provide optimal solutions which are likely to be easily generalizable to the two-variable case. Attempts to introduce specific utility functions also involve a considerable increase in complexity even if the simplest functional forms are used.

One important result of this chapter is that the form of the transport cost function plays a key role once we allow frequency to become a variable. Models in which transport costs are proportional to the bundle size (the case usually assumed in urban economics) yield completely unsatisfactory results and must be abandoned for models where the transport cost is fixed with respect to bundle size. This result also implies that we cannot write demand as a function of the delivered price, as is usually done. Instead a more complex function emerges in which mill prices and per unit transport costs do not have the same relationship to quantity demanded.

In all models the role of the two main forces on the optimum frequency of shopping is then clear—higher transport (order) costs reduce frequency and higher inventory costs act as a brake and tend to increase frequency. The generalization to two goods, where there can be joint economies of purchasing more than one good on a trip, gives the transport cost element a key role in producing differential frequencies, as we shall see in the next chapter.

3

OPTIMAL FREQUENCIES IN THE TWO-GOOD SINGLE-CENTRE CASE

It is important to remind ourselves that the reason for studying the choice of frequency is to establish whether different frequencies for purchasing different goods will ever be chosen by a consumer in preference to always buying all goods at the same frequency and on the same occasions. We also wish to establish the conditions under which multi-purpose trips will be undertaken in preference to purely single-purpose trips. The dual requirement, to show that single-purpose trips are not always optimal but that purely multi-purpose trips are also not always optimal, lies at the heart of our attempt to establish a form of consumer behaviour that is both plausible and consistent with the hierarchical structure of central place theory.

The analysis in this chapter continues to be confined to the single-centre case since we need to establish that the possibility of a mixed frequency shopping programme being optimal is independent of the structure of shopping centres available (it being of limited benefit to prove that hierarchical structure leads to differential frequency since we wish to argue that it is the possibility of differential frequency that permits a hierarchical structure to evolve). Also, it will become clear that the simultaneous analysis of choice over frequency and location is so involved that it is much more helpful to build the analysis one step at a time. Finally, it should be noted that we confine nearly all our remarks to the two-good case. Once the principles for analysing this case have been established then it is straightforward but cumbersome to deal with even more general cases. At the same time the critical question of whether mixed frequency programmes can be optimal will be settled if this turns out to be a possibility in the two-good case (as it does).

Although, as we have shown in Chapter 2, it is possible in the single-good case to construct models of the choice of frequency of shopping which take account of many factors, this is altogether a more difficult problem in the two-good case. To anticipate the analysis, it is evident that there may be an economy of scale with multi-purpose trips—the transport cost of buying two goods on the same trip need not be the sum of the transport costs of buying the goods on separate trips. This discrete jump in the cost function, which is, however, a central aspect of the model, presents such difficulties for solution that it is necessary to keep all other aspects of the model as simple as possible. Accordingly, we take the simplest cost structure and put this into a cost-minimizing framework with fixed value requirements. We saw in Chapter 2 that the qualitative aspects of the optimal solutions for frequency and bundle size were very similar for utility maximization and cost minimization in the single-good case. The feature that will be lost is the possibility of substitution between goods as the price of one rises relative to the other—a fixed value requirement for each good would presumably be consistent only with a very special form of the utility function. Were costs other than purchase costs unimportant then a constant elasticity (Bergson-type) utility function would generate fixed value requirements. The more important the other costs become (order and inventory costs), the required utility function would be less like the Bergson function. The loss of generality involved in this approach would seem to be worthwhile, since it enables us to obtain a solution to the two-good optimum frequency problem.

COST-MINIMIZING MODEL FOR FREQUENCY (STANDARD CASE)

We begin the analysis by outlining the rules for the operation of the inventory in the two-good case. A typical inventory/time graph is shown in Figure 3.1. Here we show good 1 with larger bundle sizes and higher frequency (which will probably occur if the value requirement for good 1 is higher than that for good 2). We note that there may be instances when both goods could be purchased on the same trip and others when the trips might be single purpose. We must now make clear our assumptions about the rules for operating the inventory. For the present we assume that:

(i) there are never any shortages;
(ii) the orders are never placed for a good before the inventory is empty of that good;

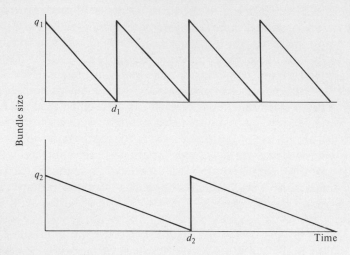

Fig. 3.1 Inventory levels for two goods over time

(iii) consumption of each good takes place at a uniform rate (expressed in value terms);
(iv) the 'carrying' cost of the inventory is proportional to the value of stock per unit time held in the inventory;
 (v) the intervals between successive purchases of a given good are constant.

These assumptions, which are parallel to those for the single-good case, are not all as innocuous as they seem. Indeed assumption (v), which can be proved to be optimal in the single-good case is no longer so in the many-good case, and later in the chapter we investigate a model with varying bundle size and durations. Assumption (ii) continues to correspond to optimal behaviour for a world without uncertainty (since the same number of trips with smaller orders could attain with lower cost a position of not ordering before the inventory is empty). Assumptions (i) and (iv) are innocuous, but assumption (iii) could also be expressed as a requirement in physical terms. Although these are roughly equivalent in the single-good case (with the fixed value model being closer to that of a utility-maximizing framework) they can diverge in a two-good two-centre case where one good can be purchased at higher or lower prices.

The one aspect of the model which does not carry over immediately from the single-good to the two-good case is that of the transport (order) cost. The exact nature of the relationship between the total order cost of a trip and the number of goods purchased on that trip turns out to be critical for our purposes. We have argued strongly that transport costs should be taken as invariant with respect to the bundle size in the single-good case because not only did the model of proportionality give implausible results, but the assumption that the bus fare or time taken was proportional to bundle size seemed unrealistic. However, in buying more than one good on a trip to a given centre, not only will there be a larger bundle to be transported but also the shopper will have to visit more than one shop and will have to increase the amount of time taken over shopping. This suggests that there are three possible cases for the structure of the order (transport) cost element:

(a) order costs are strictly proportional to the number of goods purchased on a trip;
(b) order costs per trip are invariant with respect to the number of goods purchased but are incurred only if a trip is made;
(c) order costs contain both a fixed element and an element proportional to the number of goods purchased on the trip.

The first two cases can be dealt with very briefly and the bulk of the chapter is then directed to a thorough analysis of the third case.

(a) ORDER COSTS PROPORTIONAL TO THE NUMBER OF GOODS PURCHASED

Suppose firstly that order costs are proportional purely to the number of goods purchased. This would correspond to a model in which there was a time cost of visiting a shop (shopping cost) but no cost of getting to the centre (travel cost). Not only is this very implausible but the results of incorporating it into our basic inventory model are very unsatisfactory. The lack of any shared costs of buying the two goods means that the optimal frequencies for buying the two goods are independently determined and that there are no multi-purpose trips except by accident.

Using case (a*) of Chapter 2 as the starting point for our formal investigations, and noting that there are two value requirements, V_2 and V_2, we can obtain the optimal frequencies

$$f_1^* = \surd(cV_1/\tau), \qquad (3.1)$$

$$f_2^* = \sqrt{(cV_2/\tau)} \qquad\qquad (3.2)$$

where τ is the shopping cost of visiting a shop.

Frequency is higher for the good with the greater value requirement. Even if f_1^* and f_2^* have no common factors, there must be a repeating cycle with a day on which both goods are purchased every $d_1^* d_2^*$ days. However, this may lead to a very low number of multi-purpose trips and is certainly not in the spirit of the literature which has criticized the single-purpose trip assumption.

(b) ORDER COSTS INVARIANT TO THE NUMBER OF GOODS PURCHASED

The second case is more interesting since it corresponds to the assumption used in one interpretation of the multi-good allocation model developed by Bacon (1971). It would be generated by a situation in which travel to the centre costs money or time (travel cost) but in which visiting a shop is costless. It will be shown in Chapter 4 that if frequencies are fixed in such a model then multi-purpose trips will often be optimal if there is a hierarchical structure of shopping centres. Models using this cost assumption have been analysed in classical inventory theory and Naddor (1966) presents a powerful general argument which shows that in the single-centre case all frequencies would be set equal. Suppose that the frequencies were not equal and then consider the good purchased at the lower frequency. If we increased its frequency to that of the other good we should make a double saving in costs. First, we should save on any transport costs for trips on which the lower-frequency good was bought and the higher-frequency good was not (if the higher frequency were not an integer multiple of the lower) and we should not increase transport costs since the higher-frequency trips are already paid for (two goods costing the same as one per trip). Second, by increasing the frequency we should lower bundle size and hence decrease inventory costs. Hence all frequencies in the cost-minimizing solution must be equal. Exactly the same result would hold within a utility-maximizing framework. This model gives a strong reason for the existence of multi-purpose trips but would never permit a mixed frequency shopping programme. All trips in a many-centre case (with no price differentials) would be made to the nearest centre selling all goods, and lower-order centres would do no trade. Clearly, the assumption of pure fixed order costs to shopping is not consistent with the existence of a hierarchical structure of centres.

(c) ORDER COSTS WITH A FIXED COST AND A COST PROPORTIONAL TO THE NUMBER OF GOODS PURCHASED

The generalization of the two special cases has both a fixed element (travel cost) and a variable element (shopping cost) proportional to the number of goods purchased. Such models have been very briefly discussed in the literature. Indeed Reinhardt (1973), in his pioneering paper, makes exactly this assumption and Naddor (1966) also discusses such a model. However, neither author gives a full analysis of the operation of a model with such a cost structure and indeed both treatments leave something to be desired. Both authors attempt to restrict the problem by assuming that the higher frequency of purchase will be an integer multiple of that of the lower frequency. Reinhardt indeed (p. 499) argues for equal frequencies: 'Suppose the household runs out of, say, toothpaste between consecutive trips and a special trip is made to secure only that one item. This trip is an irrational act, because had he picked up this item on the previous trip, he would have incurred the smaller holding cost for the item only, and not the higher procurement cost of the trip.' This is exactly Naddor's argument for equal frequencies in the pure fixed order cost model. What it ignores is that in buying toothpaste more frequently there will be the additional shopping cost aspect to bear even though there is no extra transport cost element. Hence the saving in inventory costs will possibly be balanced by the increased shopping costs.

Naddor is mathematically more sophisticated—he assumes the frequencies stand in an integer multiple relationship (without justification) and then optimizes over the lower frequency as a continuous variable, trying different integer multiples for the two frequencies and then choosing the lowest cost combination. Finally, the optimal frequency over this set is rounded to an integer value, since it scarcely seems sensible to order (say) every 1.3 days. The problem here is twofold. First, this technique does not necessarily obtain the optimal value defined solely over integer values of frequency, since it is not necessarily true that the nearest integer to the optimum unrestricted solution has the lowest value over all integers. Second, it is not proved that the two frequencies must stand in an integer multiple relationship. Indeed, it is shown later in this chapter that once frequencies are restricted to integer values then the two frequencies at the optimum need not be in an integer multiple relationship to each other. This property seems likely to hold over the optimization in continuous space.

In what follows we need first to derive the cost functions for the two separate cases where the functions have frequencies standing in an integer multiple relationship and where they do not. There is no single function that is valid in both situations (which is a function solely of the two frequencies). A further restriction that we place upon the problem is that the frequencies (durations) are themselves integer. Since the basic time unit can be as short as a day this is not a very restrictive assumption. It also seems realistic to limit ourselves to patterns repeating over whole numbers of days— it scarcely seems likely that shopping would actually take place every 1.3 days since there are too many other integer constraints on behaviour to permit this. At the same time the analysis is not made more difficult by abandoning the possibility of frequency being a continuous variable because discreteness has already been introduced by the switches in the cost function that occur when the two frequencies are in an integer multiple relationship. Rather than work with frequencies it is much easier to think in terms of the durations (d) between successive purchases. First, we obtain a solution for the case where the longer duration (which we label as good 2) is an integer multiple of the shorter duration. Since d_2 is an exact integer multiple of d_1 then it is possibly every d_2 days to make one multi-purpose trip. Within the same period it is also necessary to make $(d_2/d_1) - 1$ trips for good 1. This means that the total cost per period when d_2 is an integer multiple of d_1 is

$$TC_I = \frac{t + 2\tau}{d_2} + \frac{\{(d_2/d_1) - 1\}\{t + \tau\}}{d_2} + cV_1 d_1 + cV_2 d_2 + V_1 + V_2 \qquad (3.3)$$

$$= \frac{t + \tau}{d_1} + \frac{\tau}{d_2} + cV_1 d_1 + cV_2 d_2 + V_1 + V_2 \qquad (3.4)$$

for $d_2 = kd_1$ where $k = 1, 2, 3, \ldots$, and d_i are integer.

When the durations are not in an integer multiple relationship then every d_1d_2 days the two cycles overlap and one multi-purpose trip can be made. However, if d_1 and d_2 have an (integer) highest common factor (HCF) greater than unity there will be other occasions for multi-purpose trips. Consider buying good 1 every four days and good 2 every six days. Not only every twenty-four days but also every twelve days is there a coincidence of the two cycles. In general, if h is the highest common factor there are h multi-purpose trips, and $(d_2 - h)$ single-purpose trips for good 1 and $(d_1 - h)$ single-purpose trips for good 2 every (d_1d_2) days. Total costs are

$$TC_N = \frac{(t + 2\tau)h + (d_1 + d_2 - 2h)(t + \tau)}{d_1d_2}$$

$$+ cV_1d_1 + cV_2d_2 + V_1 + V_2 \qquad (3.5)$$

for $d_2 = kd_1$ where $k \neq 1, 2, 3, \ldots$, h is HCF of d_1, d_2 ($\neq d_1$), and d_i are integer. We can see that equation (3.5) includes equation (3.4) as a special case where h is equal to d_1. However, it is clear that the function (3.5) is not continuous in d_1 and d_2 but has various discontinuities depending on whether h is 1, 2, 3, $\ldots$, etc. As the appendix to this chapter makes clear, the case when the durations have an integer multiple relationship ($h = d_1$) allows a particularly simple analysis because of certain special properties of equation (3.4). Accordingly, we keep the expressions separate.

The technical problem we face is to find the values of d_1 and d_2 that minimize equations (3.4) or (3.5) subject to the feasibility restrictions. The nature of the problem with both functions defined on (integer) lattices makes it clear that differential calculus type arguments will not be available and that some form of discrete optimization will be needed. It should be noted that this difficulty arises even before we insist that the d_i are integer because of the switch in the function for integer multiple pairs of the d_i caused by the fixed cost being shared over a greater or lesser proportion of trips per period. The use of discrete optimization in turn makes it impossible to find an analytical solution for the optimum. What we are able to give is a technique for generating a *finite* list of necessary and sufficient conditions to show that a given combination is optimal. Since it also turns out that this list is usually quite short for most solutions this is an enormous gain on the enumerative approach, which would calculate the value of the function at every point (for a given set of parameter values) and then choose the smallest. The conditions we generate are necessary and sufficient in the following sense that, whatever the parameter values (t, τ, c, V_1, and V_2), they are the maximal set that will ever be required (although for particular parameter values some will be non-binding and hence redundant) and that if they hold no other condition is required (i.e. they imply all other conditions).

The idea used is essentially one derived from parametric programming. If a certain parameter condition needs to hold in order for a particular combination of variables to be optimal then if it (just) does not hold a different combination is optimal. Hence there is in parameter space a boundary between these two solution combinations. We are aiming to identify all such boundaries. This idea is used again in Chapter 5 to determine the market areas of various centres in the fixed frequency case. Once we have developed a technique of identifying the optimum for all parameter values we can turn to the question of examining what happens as we vary the distance parameter t, since it is this which essentially discriminates between centres for consumers. Such an approach is feasible because of the finite number of variable combinations that we could be interested in.

The proof of the algorithm for generating the inequalities which have to be satisfied in order for a combination to be optimal is somewhat involved and so is given instead in the appendix to this chapter. Table 3.1 gives the conditions for a few combinations. This table indicates that, for example, provided the three given inequalities are satisfied the point (1 2) will be the optimal combination whatever the parameter values. Using the techniques of the appendix we can easily extend this table as far as we need to go for any particular set of parameters. We can see that it will not in general be necessary to evaluate all the points to establish an optimum and that moreover the inequalities, once established, are always between the same pairwise cost comparisons so that the exercise does not start afresh for every set of data.

One important aspect of the solution has not yet been discussed. The values given are for the case where $V_1 > V_2$. In such a case the frequency of shopping for good 1 could never be lower than for good 2 (the duration between purchases could not be longer) since the only reason to decrease frequency is to save on transport costs relative to inventory costs, and since transport costs are symmetric between the two goods, that with the higher value requirement will place greater pressure on inventory costs and tend towards the

TABLE 3.1

*Inequalities in general form for some given combinations
of shopping duration to be optimal $(V_1 > V_2)$*

Combination		Inequalities
d_1	d_2	
1	1	$F_I(1\ 1) < F_I(1\ 2),\ F_I(2\ 2)$
1	2	$F_I(1\ 2) < F_I(1\ 1),\ F_I(1\ 3),$
		$F_I(2\ 2)$
1	3	$F_I(1\ 3) < F_I(1\ 2),\ F_I(1\ 4)$
		$F_I(3\ 3),\ F_I(2\ 2)$
		$F_I(2\ 4),\ F_N(2\ 3)$
2	2	$F_I(2\ 2) < F_I(1\ 2),\ F_I(2\ 4)$
		$F_I(1\ 1),\ F_I(1\ 3)$
		$F_I(3\ 3),\ F_N(2\ 3)$
2	3	$F_N(2\ 3) < F_I(1\ 3),\ F_I(3\ 3)$
		$F_I(2\ 2),\ F_I(2\ 4)$

(Where $F_I(x\ y)$ is the cost of durations x and y for the integer multiple relationship and $F_N(x\ y)$ is the same for non-integer multiples.)

higher frequency. Hence we label as good 1 that with the higher value requirement.

We can illustrate the calculation of the boundaries for a set of parameter values. We first notice that the solutions to equations (3.4) and (3.5) will be the same as for functions which omit the purchase values V_1, V_2. Second, it can be seen that since costs are homogeneous of degree one in money prices we can normalize as we wish. Accordingly we set $cV_1 = 4$ and $cV_2 = 1$ and we ignore the constant (which affects the value but not the location of the optimum). Table 3.2 converts the general inequalities of Table 3.1 into more specific values in the two parameters (t and τ) that are still free. From Table 3.2 we can construct a solution phase diagram as shown in Figure 3.2.

Figure 3.2 confirms that the two solution properties that we have been seeking are indeed feasible. There are several interesting features of these solutions:

(i) There are considerable regions in (t, τ) space for which differential durations and frequencies (a mixed frequency shopping programme) are optimal. We can see that, in the limited

TABLE 3.2

Inequalities in specific form for given combinations of shopping duration to be optimal $(cV_1 = 4,\ cV_2 = 1)$

Combination		Inequalities
d_1	d_2	
1	1	$\tau < 2$
		$t + 2\tau < 10$
1	2	$\tau > 2$
		$\tau < 6$
		$t + \tau < 8$
1	3	$\tau > 6$
		$\tau < 12$
		$t + \tau < 12$
		$3t + 2\tau < 18$
		$6t + 7\tau < 60$
		$2t + 3\tau < 24$
2	2	$t + \tau > 8$
		$\tau < 8$
		$t + 2\tau > 10$
		$3t + 2\tau > 18$
		$t + 2\tau < 30$
		$t - \tau > 6$
2	3	$2t + 3\tau > 24$
		$2t + \tau < 24$
		$t - \tau < 6$
		$2t + \tau < 12$

region evaluated, the combinations (1 2), (1 3), and (2 3) can all be optimal for certain frequencies. The relative size of these regions will vary with the other parameters which are here in the fixed ratio of values of four to one.

(ii) Non-integer multiple combinations can indeed be optimal. The combination (2 3) illustrates this possibility and indicates that, certainly for integer frequencies, the analysis of Naddor and Reinhardt is incomplete.

(iii) For a given value of τ, as the value of t increases, the optimal solution changes at certain discrete values of t. Hence frequency will vary discretely with distance. There will however, in a city of homogeneous consumers, be regions of consumers all with the same frequency and the same allocation. It is this result which leads to the possibility that sufficient trade could be generated for a lower-order centre to emerge.

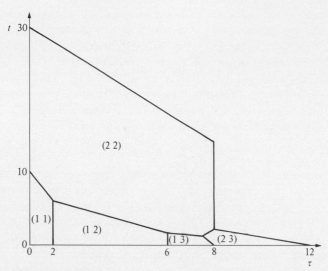

Fig. 3.2 Solution regions for the one-centre two-good variable frequency model ($cV_1 = 4$, $cV_2 = 1$)

(iv) An unexpected result is that under certain conditions, as we examine consumers further and further away from a given centre, the frequency of purchasing one of the goods may increase. There are two such examples in Figure 3.2. At the boundary between solutions (1 3) and (2 2) the frequency of buying good 1 falls from daily purchase to purchase every other day, but the purchase of good 2 rises from once every three days to once every two days. This is because the increase in distance gradually increases the benefit of joint trips relative to the inventory-related advantages of making different numbers of trips for the two goods. A similar case occurs at the boundary between solutions (2 3) and (2 2). Here the frequency of buying good 2 increases with no effect on the frequency of good 1 but the total number of shopping trips decreases very dramatically.

(v) Some consumers will make only multi-purpose trips, for example in solution regions (1 1) and (2 2), but it is extremely unlikely that this will be so for all consumers in the town unless τ is very small. If τ is small then Naddor's argument shows that all solution regions bordering the t axis must have equal frequencies and durations.

(vi) Once the optimal frequencies are known then the optimal bundle sizes follow immediately from the fixed value per period requirements. There will also be constant bundle sizes within the solution regions but discrete jumps at the boundaries.

(vii) It can be seen that for the particular values chosen some of the constraints are redundant. For example, although all six constraints bind for solution (2 2), for solution region (1 3) only three of the possible six bind. Indeed it may well be true that there is no set of parameter values when all six possible constraints bind simultaneously. Our algorithm merely generates a maximal list of those which will bind under some conditions (and omits those which will never be binding).

(viii) It is clear that in many cases the number of combinations that need to be evaluated is small and this shows that the approach is not merely feasible but also quite efficient.

This demonstration serves to confirm our central argument. There will be some consumers (possibly many) for whom a mixed frequency shopping programme will be optimal even in the presence of a single shopping centre. This makes it possible that were a second, lower-order, centre to appear it could attract enough trade to survive even though it did not sell both goods. Some of the shopping done on the single-purpose trips to the higher-order centre could be captured from consumers living sufficiently close. This indeed is the principal theme of this book, and the obvious extension of the analysis would be to turn to an integration of this consumer model (the 'demand aspect') with a location of shops model (the 'supply aspect'). However, this is such a formidable task that it would require study in its own right, and instead we investigate two lines of generalization of consumer behaviour thrown up by this analysis. The first problem is that of the generalization to three or more goods and the second is that of unequal purchase intervals.

THE MANY-GOOD CASE

Although, as we have pointed out, the two-good model establishes the main result, it is of interest to consider what would be required to generalize the model to more goods (as would be required if we wished to investigate hierarchies with more than two sizes of shopping centre). The sole difficulty is that rather than having two distinct forms for the cost function depending on whether or not the higher frequency is an integer multiple of the lower frequency, there will be many different cases. Table 3.3 lists the five cases for the three-good model. As a result, although the general techniques for

TABLE 3.3
Class of cost functions in the three-good model

1	$d_3 \, I \, d_2$	$d_2 \, I \, d_1$	$d_3 \, I \, d_1$
2	$d_3 \, I \, d_2$	$d_2 \, N \, d_1$	$d_3 \, N \, d_1$
3	$d_3 \, N \, d_2$	$d_2 \, I \, d_1$	$d_3 \, N \, d_1$
4	$d_3 \, N \, d_2$	$d_2 \, N \, d_1$	$d_3 \, N \, d_1$
5	$d_3 \, N \, d_2$	$d_2 \, N \, d_1$	$d_3 \, I \, d_1$

(Where I represents 'is an integer multiple of' and N represents 'is not an integer multiple of'.)

comparing pairs of solutions will be the same as in the two-good case, the number of comparisons required to establish optimality will be considerably greater than before. For example, to establish that the combination (1 1 1) was optimal it would be necessary to compare it with (1 1 2), (1 2 2), and (2 2 2) for the case of values in decreasing order of good number. Other cases will be correspondingly more complex.

UNEQUAL PURCHASE DURATIONS

The second extension of our basic model is the consideration of the possibility of what we term 'unequal bundle sizes'. In all the analysis so far, we have followed standard inventory theory and assumed, without proof, that on every occasion in which a given good is purchased the bundle size will be the same. This is of course equivalent to assuming equal duration between all purchases of the good. In single-good models it can be proved that such a pattern is optimal. However, it does appear to have been overlooked that, if on some occasions we are buying one good and on others two goods (thus increasing the value purchased), inventory cost considerations may tend to push us towards equalizing the total value of purchases per trip. This would lead to smaller bundles of the more frequently purchased good being bought on multi-purpose trips relative to purchases on single-purchase trips. This possibility should be taken into account in our investigation of differential frequency. It can be seen that such a possibility will, if anything, strengthen the likelihood of mixed frequency shopping programmes. If all trips were multi-purpose then nothing would be gained by varying bundle size and the cost functions we have already used in constructing Tables 3.2 and 3.3 will continue to be the lowest attainable. It may be possible, using variable bundle sizes, to reduce further costs for mixed frequency programmes (since they have been calculated for the restricted case) and, if so, this will increase the likelihood of such combinations being optimal, i.e. it would extend the range of parameter values for which they are optimal. We sketch briefly the revised cost function for the variable bundle size model. The basic inventory diagram now has to be revised to that of Figure 3.3 for the analogue to the integer multiple case.

We show the case where every d_2 periods a multi-purpose trip is made on which q_2 units of good 2 and q_{11} units of good 1 are purchased. In addition another d_{11} periods latter q_{12} units of good 1 are purchased and this is repeated after d_{12} periods. The cycle then repeats after another d_{12} periods in the same fashion. There is an important assumption embedded in this model. The rate of consumption is set at a constant value per day for each good. This determines for how long a bundle will last in the inventory. The restriction to integer values makes the solution of this model considerably easier. There are two cases based along the same lines as on previous analysis. The analogue to the integer multiple case is shown in Figure 3.3. One purchase of good 2 corresponds to one joint purchase of good 1 and n single-purpose purchases. The cost function is

$$TC_I = [(t + 2) + n(t + \tau) + d_2V_1 + d_2V_2$$
$$+ cp_1q_{11}d_{11} + ncp_1q_{12}d_{12} + cp_2q_2d_2]/d_2 \qquad (3.6)$$

where d_{11}, d_{12}, and d_2 are integer and n is integer. Also,

$$d_2 = d_{11} + nd_{12}. \qquad (3.7)$$

Finally,

$$p_1q_{11} = V_1d_{11},$$
$$p_1q_{12} = V_1d_{12}. \qquad (3.8)$$

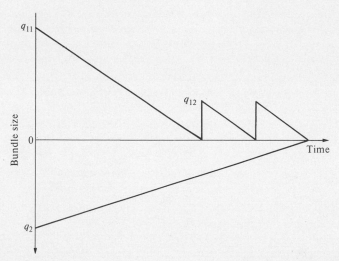

Fig. 3.3 Inventory levels for two goods with variable bundle sizes (integer multiple case)

Hence the cost function is

$$TC_I = [(t+2\tau) + \{(d_2 - d_{11})(t+\tau)\}/d_{12} + d_2 V_1 + d_2 V_2$$
$$+ cd_{11}^2 V_1 + cV_1 d_{12}(d_2 - d_{11}) + cV_2 d_2^2]/d_2 \qquad (3.9)$$

for $(d_2 - d_{11})/d_{12}$ integer. This function is feasible only for durations satisfying the restrictions. Cases where $d_{11} = d_{12}$ have effectively been analysed in the constant bundle model. Table 3.4 lists some feasible 'integer multiple'-type combinations. This table gives all the feasible 'integer multiple'-type combinations for values of d_2 up to four periods. Not only do we have the new cases, for example buying good 2 every three periods together with enough good 1 for two periods and then buying just enough good 1 to last one more period until the cycle starts again; but also attention is drawn to the fact that the cost per period of cases such as (3 1 4) is the same as (1 3 4)—it is immaterial when the large inventory is held given that the average is constant. A systematic tendency to buy less on joint trips would clearly sometimes require an additional restriction (for example more than proportionately higher carrying costs for large bundles, as suggested in Chapter 2).

If the frequencies are not of this integer multiple type then they

TABLE 3.4
*Some feasible duration patterns for the two-good
unequal bundle case*

d_{11}	d_{12}	d_2	Comment
1	0	1	Analysed as (1 1)
1	1	2	Analysed as (1 2)
2	0	2	Analysed as (2 2)
2	1	3	New case
3	0	3	Analysed as (3 3)
1	2	3	New case
1	1	3	Analysed as (1 3)
4	0	4	Analysed as (4 4)
3	1	4	New case
2	1	4	New case
2	2	4	Analysed as (2 4)
1	3	4	New case
1	1	4	Analysed as (1 4)

will follow some such pattern as that shown in Figure 3.4. The durations are linked by the equation

$$d_{11} + nd_{12} = hd_2 \qquad (3.10)$$

where h and n are integer (but h is unequal to unity).

The cost function can be derived in the usual fashion. The method of solving this case is likely to have to be more cumbersome than before since the 'integer multiple'-type case is no longer of the special type used in the basic model.[†] However, we can illustrate the effects of introducing this extra complication on the location of the solution boundaries. Consider the case with parameter values $cV_1 = 4$, $cV_2 = 1$ and $\tau = 7$. In the fixed bundle case there is a solution boundary between (1 3) and (2 2). The value of t at this boundary is obtained by equating

$$F(1\ 3) = t + 16\tfrac{1}{3},$$

$$F(2\ 2) = t/2 + 17,$$

therefore $t = 1\tfrac{1}{3}$.

[†]The algorithm given in the appendix to this chapter to solve the fixed bundle size problem makes extensive use of the fact that the integer multiple function (3.4) is additive and increases in all directions away from the minimum: equation (3.9) does not have these properties.

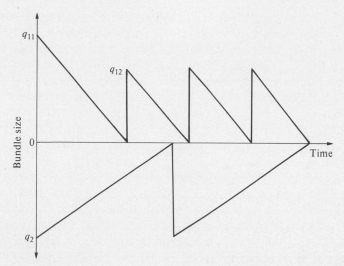

Fig. 3.4 Inventory levels for two goods with variable bundle sizes (non-integer multiple case)

If we now consider unequal bundle sizes these cases are denoted (1 1 3) and (2 0 2). We assert that the case (1 2 3) (or equivalently (2 1 3)) now interposes between these two solution regions at certain parameter values. The cost function is

$$F(1\ 2\ 3) = \tfrac{2}{3}t + 16\tfrac{2}{3}.$$

The boundary between (1 1 3) and (1 2 3) is at $t = 1$ and the boundary between (1 2 3) and (2 0 2) is at $t = 2$. This illustrates how the introduction of variable frequency is likely to shrink the solution regions for purely multi-purpose shopping programmes and to increase the number of consumers for whom a mixed frequency programme would be optimal; of course, for some consumers equal bundle sizes but different frequencies may remain optimal. This sketch does enough to show that the assumption of equal bundle size merely simplifies analysis without altering the main results.

CONCLUSION

This chapter has established the key result that for many customers in a town a mixed frequency shopping programme may be optimal. This is so whether or not bundle sizes of a given good are restricted to be the same on all occasions. Since this phenomenon of some single-purpose and some multi-purpose trips has been shown to be possible in the single-centre case the way is clear to argue that the existence of such shopping patterns allows a hierarchy of shopping centres to emerge. Moreover, since the same solutions hold for wide variations in the value of parameter t (which indexes distance between consumers and the shopping centre) it is clear that the possibility exists that many trips just for good 1 are made (despite the fact that good 2 could be bought at the same centre). This gives rise to a captive trade for a 'good 1' shop locating closer to these consumers than is the higher-order centre. Of course the emergence of a hierarchy of centres may cause frequencies for some consumers to separate even more than they would have done in the absence of the hierarchical structure. However, the analysis of this chapter makes it clear that such a separation of frequencies could not be attributed solely to the presence of the hierarchical structure. There is no danger of this being labelled as a 'chicken and egg' case.

The analysis has been carried out in detail only for the two-good, cost-minimizing 'lot size'-type model. The general conclusion will hold also for the many-good case and the variable bundle size even though a complete solution is not given for either case. For the even more general two-good, utility-maximizing model explicit conditions for particular solutions would be even harder to arrive at, not least because of the automatic increase in the number of free variables from two to three. This is because in the fixed values model the determination of optimal frequencies automatically determines the bundle sizes, whereas in the fixed income case, two frequencies and one bundle size must be known before the other bundle is determined. We therefore rely on the strong parallels at the one-good level to persuade us that similar results would also be obtained at the two-good level. A particularly important aspect of the model is the role of the two elements of transport costs. The smaller is the 'shopping' cost element the less likely are frequencies to be different. The possibility of differential frequencies and hierarchical structure rests largely on the importance of the good-specific shopping cost relative to the centre-specific transport cost.

Thus Chapters 2 and 3 have established that it is reasonable to assume that consumers, minimizing their total cost of shopping, will, in general, shop at different frequencies for different goods. Once we have accepted this assumption, which has been assumed before, for example Bacon (1971), Odland (1981), and Eaton and Lipsey (1982), but has apparently never been justified, then we can turn to the issue of where consumers shop. However, it is clear from our analysis that the choice of centre may alter frequency (since it is distance cost related) and so frequency and allocation must be determined simultaneously. This is again a difficult problem and it is easier first to look at the case where frequencies are fixed and just allocation is to be decided. Chapter 4 explains and generalizes Bacon's (1971) fixed frequency model of the allocation of shopping trips between a hierarchy of centres.

APPENDIX: AN ALGORITHM FOR SOLVING THE OPTIMAL FREQUENCIES IN A TWO-GOOD ONE-CENTRE EQUAL BUNDLE SIZE MODEL

The problem to be solved can be stated as: choose d_1 and d_2 so as to minimize total costs where costs are defined by the functions

$$F_I = \frac{(t+2\tau)+(d_2/d_1-1)(t+\tau)}{d_2} + V_1 + V_2$$

$$+ cV_1 d_1 + cV_2 d_2 \qquad (3.11)$$

if d_2 is an integer multiple of d, and

$$F_N = \frac{(t+2\tau)h+(d_1+d_2-2h)(t+\tau)}{d_1 d_2} +$$

$$V_1 + V_2 + cV_1 d_1 + cV_2 d_2 \qquad (3.12)$$

where h is the highest common factor of d_1, d_2 and d_2 is not an integer multiple of d_1. d_1 and d_2 are restricted to integer values.

We notice immediately that $(V_1 + V_2)$ can be omitted since it is a fixed cost and cannot affect the choice of optimal d_i. For simplicity we make the following notational changes:

$$d_1 = x$$
$$d_2 = y$$
$$cV_1 = \alpha$$
$$cV_2 = \beta$$

$$\therefore F_I = \frac{t+\tau}{x} + \frac{\tau}{y} + \alpha x + \beta y, \qquad (3.11^*)$$

$$F_N = \frac{t+\tau}{x} + \frac{t+\tau}{y} - \frac{th}{xy} + \alpha x + \beta y, \qquad (3.12^*)$$

x, y integer. We must also remember that these functions were derived for $y \geq x$ (i.e. $V_1 \geq V_2$) and that the reverse case can be obtained simply by relabelling the variable.

The integer restrictions mean that it is impossible to use the calculus trick of comparing the optimum with all other points simply by identifying where the derivative is zero. Instead we face the possibility of needing to compare the function at a given point with the function at all other points in order to be sure that the given point is optimal. Such a programme is infeasible in general even when only integer values are involved. Even limiting ourselves to economically plausible values would still make complete enumeration very tedious. Furthermore, the results would be informative only for the particular values of the parameters used. Our requirement is a technique that cuts down the number of comparisons to a finite and hopefully small number and which is also valid for all possible values of the parameters. The algorithm we present has both these features.

The starting point for the proof is the nature of the total cost function for the integer multiple case. Consider this function (F_I) as a function defined over a continuous field (rather than a lattice). There are three critical properties:

  (i) $F_I(x\ y) < F_N(x\ y)$ everywhere (since $h < x$ by definition).

 (ii) $F_I(x\ y)$ is an *additive* function and can be written in the form:

$$F_I(x\ y) = f(x) + g(y).$$

(iii) $F_I(x\ y)$ has a single minimum in the positive quadrant and it increases monotonically in every direction as we move away from this minimum.

From the third property it follows that if we consider a combination $(x^*\ y^*)$ in F_I and we can find points $(x^* - m\ y^*)$ and $(x^* + n\ y^*)$, both of which are greater than $(x^*\ y^*)$, then all points $(x^* - m - c\ y^*)$ and $(x^* + n + d\ y^*)$ are also greater than $(x^*\ y^*)$. Since the function increases away from the minimum along the x axis, then once we have identified a point lower than certain points on either side all points further away must be higher still.

The argument holds when the function evaluations are made solely at integer points which are also I-feasible (i.e. where one is an integer multiple of the other). A similar property would hold if we could find a pair of points on the y axis which bracket $(x^*\ y^*)$ and are both greater. The set of all points outside the bracketing pair on the y axis would then all be greater.

In Figure 3.5 the circled point (1 2) is under consideration and if all three crossed points (1 1), (2 2), and (1 3) are greater then no point on the axes running through $x=1$ or $y=2$ can be lower than (1 2). The next step in the argument is to use the additivity property. This implies that

$$f(x^*\ y^*+s) - f(x^*\ y^*) = f(x^*+t\ y^*+s) - f(x^*+t\ y^*), \quad (3.13)$$

i.e. the effect of a given change in y on the function is the same whatever the value of x (and vice versa). Hence if the point (1 4) is definitely worse than (1 2) because (1 3) is known to be greater than (1 2), then the points (2 4), (3 4), and (4 4) cannot be optimal since they are all greater than (2 3), (3 3), and (4 3) respectively. This argument taken in its general form means that once we have identified on each axis running through $(x^*\ y^*)$ points greater than it then no points outside the rectangular area running through these points can be optimal. Figure 3.6 shows such a rectangular region for the point (2 4).

For the point (2 4) we have found in each direction the nearest points on the axes through the points which have y as an integer multiple of x. Our argument has demonstrated that if (2 4) is less

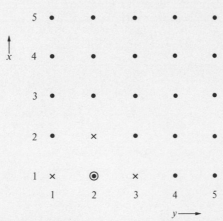

Fig. 3.5 A lattice of durations in the two-good case

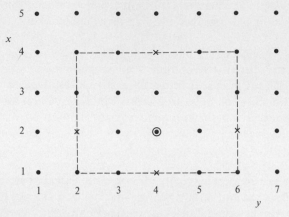

Fig. 3.6 A boundary rectangular region around (2 4)

than the four points (2 2), (2 6), (1 4), and (4 4) then it is less than
all points outside the rectangle bounded by (1 2), (1 6), (4 2), and
(4 6). Of course not all of these points are integer multiples but we
can now use our first property that the value of F_N at a point is
greater than F_I. Hence if $(x^*\ y^*)$ is less than all points in a region
evaluated on F_I (whether I-feasible or not) then it is less than all
points in that region when correctly evaluated by F_I or F_N. This then
leaves just the points on and inside the rectangle for comparison.
By our additivity argument the four points at the corners of the
rectangle must be greater on F_I, so they too cannot be optimal.
Hence all that remains is to compare all remaining points correctly
evaluated. This gives us a minimal list of conditions to be satisfied
for (2 4) to be optimal in all situations:

$$F_I\,(2\ 4) <\quad F_I\,(4\ 4),\ F_I\,(1\ 4),\ F_I\,(2\ 2),$$
$$F_I\,(2\ 6),\ F_I\,(1\ 3),\ F_I\,(1\ 5)$$
$$F_I\,(3\ 3),\ F_I\,(3\ 6),\ F_N\,(4\ 5),$$
$$F_N\,(3\ 5),\ F_N\,(2\ 5),\ F_N\,(3\ 2),$$
$$F_N\,(4\ 2),\ F_N\,(4\ 3).$$

If these conditions are satisfied then (2 4) is less than any other point.
The list of comparisons can be made even shorter since the functions
(3.11*) and (3.12*) are correctly defined only for $y \geq x$. If $x > y$ we
know that the point cannot be optimal (there is no reason to shop

more frequently for the good with the smaller value requirement). This consideration removes the last three comparisons from the list.

There is a second argument which can sometimes be used to reduce such a list still further. If it is necessary when establishing (say) that (3 3) is optimal to compare it with (1 4), then this implies that it is possible for them to be equal and optimal. If we regard this in parametric space we assert that there must be a solution boundary separating these two regions with no other region in between. Hence it is necessary in analysing the optimality of (1 4) to compare it with (3 3). However, it is easy to see that when (1 4) is optimal the point (3 3) is strictly greater, since (1 3) and (2 4) will be greater than (1 4) and these together imply that (3 3) is greater still. Thus in drawing up our list of comparisons which can be binding we can delete any that would not need to be made in the reverse test for optimality. There are no such points in the case for (2 4).

These arguments allow us to deal with all points which have y as an integer multiple of x (I-feasible), except for one complication. Some points have no neighbouring I-feasible points north or west before the restriction of $y \geq x$ is broken—these are the points with $y = x$. This means that a point such as (2 2) could be optimal even though the F_I function does not increase away from it north or westwards. The value of F_I (3 2) could be less than F_I (2 2) while the correct cost †of the combination (3 2), which we can denote F_I^* (3 2), would be greater still and certainly can never be optimal. The result of these considerations is that applying the test of increasingness can be too restrictive. Consider the point (1 1): we need to establish that F_I (1 1) $< F_I$ (1 2). We might also attempt to rule out all points in a northward direction by insisting that F_I (1 1) $< F_I$ (2 1). This is too strong. F_I (1 1) could be greater than F_I (2 1) but still less than all I-feasible points lying further north. In particular, if we do not use the latter restriction we can see that the points on the diagonal could still be less than (1 1) and hence optimal. No point off the diagonal is a direct threat since additivity has shown that all rightward movements are cost-increasing. Hence we are left with comparing F_I (1 1) with F_I (n n) for all n. However, additivity

---

† Remembering that the cost functions have been derived on the assumption that $y \geq x$, i.e. that the single-purpose trips are for good x; if $y < x$ then the cost function should allow single-purpose trips for good y instead.

and the increasing nature of the function imply that if the function increases along any straight line it will continue to increase along the extension of that line. Hence if $F_I(1\ 1) < F_I(2\ 2)$ it is less than F_I $(n\ n)$ for all n. This argument completes the algorithm for I-feasible points and we must now turn to N-feasible points (where y is a non-integer multiple of x).

Again, the additivity and increasingness of F_I make the establishment of the optimality of an N-feasible point fairly straightforward. For an N-feasible point to be optimal it must be less than the nearest I-feasible points on the axes passing through it. If it is less than these points it is then less than all points lying outside the rectangle joining these points, since the point in question evaluated on F_I will be less still and hence *all* points outside the rectangle will be higher evaluated on F_I. *A fortiori*, those which are N-feasible will be even greater when evaluated correctly on F_N. Hence we need merely to check the other points on and inside the rectangle (excluding the corner points). Consider the N-feasible point (3 4)—it has neighbouring I-feasible points (2 4), (4 4), (3 3), and (3 6). It then follows that for overall optimality of (3 4) we must establish:

$$F_N\ (3\ 4) < \quad F_I\ (2\ 4),\ F_I\ (4\ 4),\ F_I\ (3\ 3),$$
$$F_I\ (3\ 6),\ F_N\ (2\ 5),\ F_N\ (3\ 5),$$
$$F_N\ (4\ 5).$$

The same arguments on reverse comparisons can often be used to reduce the list still further. It can be seen that the difficulty of nonexistence of N-feasible points to the north or west does not occur since the diagonal points $(n\ n)$ always bound N-feasible points in those directions.

The procedure for establishing the minimal list of inequalities that must hold for a given combination to be optimal can be summarized by the following rules:

1. For *I*-feasible points

(a) *For non-diagonal points* $(y > x)$

(i) Determine the nearest I-feasible points on the axis running through the point in question. No point outside the rectangle running through these four points need be compared, nor need the four corner points be compared.

(ii) Compare the point with these four points and with all other points on or inside the rectangle (excluding the corners) using the appropriate cost function. Delete any comparisons that would be ruled out by an application of (i) to the optimality of the point in question.

(*b*) *For diagonal points*

(i) Determine the nearest *I*-feasible points on the axes passing through the point in east and south directions. No point outside the two sides of the rectangle running through these points need be considered, nor need the corner point.

(ii) Compare the point with all points inside the rectangle (excluding the corner) evaluated using the appropriate cost functions and also compare the point with the neighbouring points on the diagonal using the F_I function. Delete any comparisons that would be ruled out by an application of (i) to the optimality of the point in question.

2. For *N*-feasible points

(i) Determine the nearest *I*-feasible points on the axes running through the point in question. No point outside the rectangle joining those four points or the four corners of the rectangle need be compared with the point in question.

(ii) Compare the point with all points on or inside the rectangle (excluding the corner points) using the appropriate cost functions. Delete any comparisons that would be ruled out by an application of (i) to the optimality of the point in question.

The comparisons generated by these rules are a maximal set that could be required under any circumstances which are necessary and sufficient for the point in question to be optimal. It is evident that the properties of F_I, being both increasing away from the minimum and additive, allow a tremendous reduction in the number of comparisons that need to be made. Further, it is clear that the same list of inequalities is used whatever the parameter values, so that once the list has been determined for any combination the task does not have to be undertaken again. Also, it is in practice unlikely that very large values of d_i will be feasible, so that it is sensible to start with the smallest values and only calculate the inequalities for larger values if this proves necessary.

4

THE ALLOCATION OF SHOPPING TRIPS WITH FIXED FREQUENCIES

We begin by considering the shopping problem that might confront a typical household in a small town. There are two shopping centres from which to choose: the town centre which sells everything needed in normal circumstances, and a small group of 'local' shops selling merely those goods purchased most often. To make the problem even more concrete we consider just two 'goods'—groceries and meat. The local shops, then, do not sell meat but do sell all other foodstuffs, while the town centre includes a butcher as well as a grocer. We assume that the household shops for groceries more frequently than it does for meat (perhaps three times a week for the former but twice a week for the latter), and we further assume that these frequencies are independent of the choice of centres open to the household (for example even if there were a butcher locally which the household used it would still shop for meat just twice a week) or of the prices charged. This is a strong assumption and will be relaxed in Chapter 6, but makes for analytical convenience at this stage.

The second assumption that we make about the household is that the amount of a good bought per week is independent of where it is bought. This effectively means that we are assuming zero price elasticity of demand. Such an assumption has often been used as a starting point in various studies in location theory, for example Hotelling (1929) and Eaton and Lipsey (1982), and is indeed difficult to generalize, as we have seen. A related and very important assumption is that the amount of a good purchased on any trip (the 'bundle' size) is independent of where it is purchased. This would rule out the possibility of the household making one trip to the town centre when virtually the whole week's groceries were purchased and making two other trips to the local shops to make relatively small purchases. Since such behaviour would appear to be not uncommon (because of the price advantages offered by the shops at the town centre), the lack of differential bundle sizes can be seen as an important shortcoming. As a related point we can see that it would be interesting to see whether the spatial structure that our model generates is capable of explaining the existence of price differentials between shops selling the same class of good.

The next assumption made is that the household chooses its purchasing pattern so as to minimize the total money costs of shopping per week. This important behavioural postulate means that such considerations as the time taken to travel to the shops or the inconvenience of shopping (from carrying goods) are irrelevant to the choice made. In earlier studies such factors have been largely ignored but, as has been shown in Chapter 2, they can have an important role in explaining shopping frequency.

One final assumption is needed before the problem can be solved. This is the assumption of flexible scheduling for all purchases. Within the basic time period (assumed for convenience to be a week) the various purchases are arranged at intervals so as to be of the maximum benefit to the consumer. For example, if we consider the six shopping days the sequence of purchases for the two goods could be as described by either (a) or (b) in Table 4.1. Clearly, the arrangement in (b) increases the number of days on which the two goods could be purchased on the same trip. The potential gain from such multi-purpose trips is a central part of the model but does of course imply that within the week there may be uneven intervals between

TABLE 4.1

Two weekly shopping patterns

(a) Weekly shopping patterns with regular frequencies

	Day	1	2	3	4	5	6
Good 1		P	0	P	0	P	0
Good 2		P	0	0	P	0	0

(b) Weekly shopping patterns with maximum multi-purpose trips

	Day	1	2	3	4	5	6
Good 1		P	0	P	0	P	0
Good 2		P	0	P	0	0	0

(P = good purchased, 0 = good not purchased.)

successive purchases of the same good. This formulation of the problem is perhaps less satisfactory than that of Chapter 2, where equal purchase intervals for each good are assumed. It does have the effect of allowing the simplest treatment of the spatial aspect of the problem accordingly we retain it for the present.

This assumption raises the problem of the relationship between purchasing and consuming. If the consumer were to purchase enough to last just until the next trip then uneven intervals between trips would imply unequal bundle sizes (which we have ruled out for the present). The way out of this is to recognize the role of inventories in the household's behaviour. On day one we could imagine the household buying (say) 3 units of meat. This is consumed at a rate of 1 unit per day and hence on day three, when another 3 units are purchased, the household still has 1 unit left unconsumed and this total of 4 units lasts until the end of the week when the cycle is repeated again. The costs and benefits of operating an inventory system in this way and the optimal strategy of doing so are clearly related to the determination of optimal frequencies of shopping, and have been analysed in Chapter 2. For the present, we merely assume that the inventory is being run so as to minimize the other costs of shopping but that there are no money costs to running the inventory which could vary depending on the allocation.

We next turn explicitly to the costs of shopping. There are just two categories:

 (i) the price of the good at the shop ('mill' price);
(ii) the transport costs of visiting a centre and purchasing goods there.

Our discussion of shops and goods so far has not emphasized the point that we are obviously considering 'baskets' of individual items—we label the many items of grocery as the single good 'grocery'. The definition of this composite good is, then, the average basket bought at a shop selling these items. In reality there are difficulties, since often shops of different categories (judged by their main activities) sell the same item. We cannot deal with such complications and have to imagine rather distinct types of shop. In such a case the basket of representative purchases can be valued, and this gives a 'price'. In the most general case that we will consider later in this chapter, allowance will be made for the existence of price differentials, but we will start by assuming that the same price is charged for a given good at every shop which sells it. Furthermore, we shall assume throughout that there are no quantity discounts, so that total expenditure will be strictly proportional to price.

The modelling of transport costs is more problematical. In location theory there have been two very distinct assumptions made:

(i) the literature associated with Hotelling has assumed that the total transport cost of shopping at a centre has been directly proportional to the distance of the centre from the home and to the quantity of goods purchased (usually indexed by value);
(ii) studies associated with Christaller's (1966) central place theory have suggested that transport costs are proportional to distance but are invariant with respect to the amounts purchased and transported.

These two assumptions have very different implications with regard to optimum frequency of shopping, as we have seen. However, for the present it is sufficient to attempt to justify the use of the assumption that transport costs are independent of quantity. Models in which quantity is important are largely derived from industrial location theory where it is clearly more expensive to carry 10 tons of coal for 1 mile than to carry 1 ton for 1 mile. In retail economies, however, it is scarcely plausible to suggest that a bus trip to a centre, or even a car trip, will cost more if the housewife brings back two shopping bags rather than one. Of course it is true that it may be much more inconvenient to walk or cycle with a large quantity of shopping, but it must be emphasized that at this stage we are concerned purely with money costs and these we can reasonably assume to be quantity invariant.

The exact relation between transport costs and distance we will leave open for the present, except to insist that such costs are an increasing function of the distance between the home and the centre. We define as 'home' the point from which the consumer begins the shopping trip, combined with the return trip to wherever is the final destination. Most trips begin and finish from the house and so the total cost is that of the return trip between the house and the shopping centre in question. For those shoppers who work, the trip may be from the office to the shops and back. There is one category of trip that is assumed not to be utilized—the 'cross-country' trip. The model does not allow for a consumer who leaves the house, travels to centre A to purchase some goods, then travels on to centre B to purchase some other goods, and then travels back home. If the consumer needs to visit centres A and B it is assumed that two separate trips will be made. It is felt that the gain in generality from allowing for this relatively unusual pattern would not justify the great increase in complexity that would be necessary to handle all possible cases.

The model so far described is that of Bacon's (1971) paper. In that paper the model was formalized and a method of solution suggested. However, although a proof was sketched for the optimality of the solution found, the algorithm suggested was not formally shown to converge in a finite number of steps† and cannot properly be said to have solved the problem. This difficulty was removed by Evans (1972) who showed how to recast the model as a linear programming problem. Since algorithms to solve the linear programme (LP) are known to exist (of which the so-called 'simplex' method is the best-known) it follows that the model has a solution which can be obtained in a finite number of steps irrespective of its complexity.

Before we formalize the model and show how it can be cast as an LP, it is instructive to consider a simple example that can be solved by verbal argument. Let us consider the case of three goods and two centres (labelled A and B). Centre A (local shops) sells just goods 1 and 2, while B sells all three goods. The frequencies of purchase per time period of the goods are $f(1)$, $f(2)$, and $f(3)$ and the costs of transportation to the centres are $t(A)$ and $t(B)$. The purchase prices of the goods (identical at the two centres) are $p(1)$, $p(2)$, and $p(3)$. In our particular case we are assuming that $t(A) < t(B)$ and that $f(1) > f(2) > f(3)$. The goods supplied at all centres are those most frequently purchased, while those sold only at the main shopping centre are least frequently purchased.

We can start the solution by noting that the consumer must make $f(3)$ trips to centre B to buy good 3 (there being no other source of supply). On these trips it is clearly optimal to buy goods 1 and 2 as well since they cost exactly the same at both centres and no extra

---

† Eaton and Lipsey (1982) confuse solution by algorithm with numerical simulation when they say, incorrectly, that (p. 60) '. . . to solve the consumer's problem [Bacon] was forced to rely on numerical simulation techniques'.

transport cost is required. It is here that we see the force of the assumption that transport costs are independent of quantity—once one good is purchased then however many other goods are purchased, the transport cost is fixed. Thus we see that there is an 'external' economy from the necessary trips to buy good 3. However, since $f(1)$ and $f(2)$ are larger than $f(3)$, not all purchases of goods 1 and 2 can be made on these multi-purpose trips to centre B. Since purchase prices are the same the consumer, in fact, is concerned purely with transport costs and it is evident that he will make another $f(2) - f(3)$ trips to centre A to buy good 2 and of course will buy good 1 at the same time. There will be a final $f(1) - f(2)$ trips to centre A—on which just good 1 is purchased. We finish with the allocation:

$f(3)$ trips to B buying all 3 goods,
$f(3) - f(2)$ trips to A buying goods 1 and 2,
$f(2) - f(1)$ trips to A buying good 1.

Two features emerge from this:

(i) not all trips are to the nearest centre selling the good (even though there is no price advantage);
(ii) one particular good may be purchased at more than one centre.

The differential frequency accounts here for the second phenomenon and shows clearly how it is required to permit the existence of the hierarchical structure. If all frequencies were equal (but multi-purpose trips were possible) then the existence of the external economy generated by those goods sold at the main centre but nowhere else would lead to all shopping being carried out at this centre. The sub-centre could only be used if the model somehow generated single-purpose trips.

The method of solution outlined here would be very simple to use if centres were always arranged by distance in a pure hierarchical structure for all consumers. In fact this will not be true for two reasons:

(i) Sometimes the pattern of shops will not be able to be arranged in a strictly increasing hierarchy irrespective of distances. We show such a case in Table 4.2 and note that this can generate an additional complexity of a 'joint' economy which requires a further calculation to reach the optimum allocation.

(ii) In order to use this sequential method it was necessary that the centres were ordered by distance from the home in the same way as they would be ordered in terms of the increasing range of goods sold. Clearly, this cannot be true for all households in a town—some people will live nearest to the largest centre etc. A method of solution is needed which allows for any pattern of the range of goods supplied and relative distances from the home.

To show the typical complication that can arise when centres are not ordered in a strict hierarchy we replace the previous example by a four-centre three-good case as shown in Table 4.2. The centres are ordered by distance (increasing), with frequency decreasing with the good number. As before, $f(3)$ trips can be made to centre D on which all three goods are purchased. The consumer now has a choice—he can either make trips to centre C buying both goods 1 and 2 or he can make separate trips to centres A and B buying one

TABLE 4.2
Availability of goods in a four-centre three-good case

	Good	1	2	3
Centre	A	1	0	0
Centre	B	0	1	0
Centre	C	1	1	0
Centre	D	1	1	1

good on each trip. The costs of buying 1 unit of 1 and 2 will be either $t(A) + t(B)$ or $t(C)$. Hence depending on the relative magnitudes the consumer will make $f(3) - f(2)$ trips to C (buying both goods) or $f(3) - f(2)$ trips to A (buying good 1) and the same number of trips to B (buying good 2). In either case a further $f(2) - f(1)$ trips will be made to centre A in order to buy the final units of good 1. This example shows a new consideration—that of the 'joint' trip; centre C would not be used if it sold just one of either goods 1 or 2, but by selling both it may be able to attract trade from other centres nearer to the consumer. Whether or not the joint economy is utilized depends on the relative magnitudes of the transport costs, and this shows that it is necessary to put a (cardinal) value on these costs. Purely ordinal values (i.e. $t(A) < t(B) < t(C)$ etc.) are not sufficient to yield a definite solution.

A further feature of such models, which can be seen from elementary considerations, is that multiple solutions are quite likely. Consider the availability matrix shown in Table 4.3 where $t(A) < t(B) < t(C)$. Now $f(3)$ trips must be made to centre C to buy good 3 and $f(2)$ trips to centre B to buy good 2. Both give rise to 'external' economies for the purchase of good 1. If the total requirement for good 1 was less than the sum of these two (i.e. $f(1) < (f(2) + f(3))$) then not all external economies available will be used and there will be more than one allocation possible at the same cost. Relocating one purchase of good 1 from centre B to centre C or vice versa will not affect the total transport costs.

The tie between these various solutions can be resolved by the rule used in Bacon's (1971) paper—that between allocations of equal transport cost that one should be chosen in which each good is purchased from as near to the home as possible. The rationalization for this rule was that there is a cost (perhaps non-monetary) to the inconvenience of carrying shopping home which the consumer is also concerned to minimize. Such costs were assumed to be very small in relation to transport costs and so to affect the allocation only in these tied situations. There are a number of objections to this approach:

(i) Such costs may be small compared to the level of transport costs but they cannot be guaranteed to be small relative to the marginal advantages considered when joint economies occur. For example, we had to compare $t(A) + t(B)$ with $t(C)$, and here inconvenience costs could easily affect the allocation in such a case, however small they were relative to the general level of transport costs.

(ii) Once the idea of the disutility of shopping is introduced it would be more satisfactory to incorporate it starting from first

TABLE 4.3

Availability matrix for a three-centre three-good case

	Good	1	2	3
Centre	A	1	0	0
Centre	B	1	1	0
Centre	C	1	0	1

(1 = good available, 0 = not available.)

principles with a consumer utility function—consumers might be willing to trade inconveniences against other factors.

It seems that the tie-breaking rule is better not invoked and that we should accept the possibility of multiple solutions (which in any case are less likely when we move to more general models with price differentials).

We now turn to a mathematical formulation of the model which has been outlined in this section.

(a) A MODEL OF ALLOCATION WITHOUT PRICE DIFFERENTIALS

The general case of even this very restricted model is clearly potentially very complicated and requires a technique of solution that is guaranteed always to find the optimum allocation of shopping trips. We introduce some notation. For a given consumer let:

$t(i)$ = the transport cost of visiting centre i irrespective of how many goods are purchased there $(i = 1 \ldots I)$,

$f(ij)$ = the number of trips made to centre i to buy good j $(j = 1 \ldots J)$,

$n(j)$ = total number of trips per period on which good j must be purchased,

$f(iZ)$ = maximise $(f(i1), f(i2), \ldots f(iJ))$, all i,

$k(ij)$ = 1 if $j = Z$, $\left.\begin{array}{c} \\ \\ \end{array}\right\} i$

= 0 otherwise

The consumer's problem is then to choose the $f(ij)$ so as to minimize

$$\sum_i \sum_j t(i).f(ij).k(ij) \qquad (4.1)$$

subject to the requirements that

$$\sum_i f(ij) = n(j), \text{ all } j \qquad (4.2)$$

given $t(i)$ and $n(j)$. This form of the model, first given by Bacon (1971), we call model I. The formulation has omitted prices completely but as we have already seen, if prices are the same everywhere they cannot affect the decision as to where to buy the various goods and hence can be omitted in the optimization procedure.

The introduction of the artificial $f(iZ)$ variables is a device to make sure that transport costs are invariant with respect to the number of goods purchased on a trip. The largest frequency of purchases between goods at a centre defines the maximum number of trips that need to be made to that centre, while if the centre is not used then there is no associated transport cost. This type of structure, which occurs frequently in the operations analysis literature, is known as a fixed charge and usually needs to be handled by the advanced techniques of integer programming.

In order to overcome this difficulty Evans reformulated the problem. He added two new variables:

$f(i)$ = total number of trips to centre,
$b(ij)$ = 1 if good is sold at centre,
= 0 otherwise

$(\therefore f(i) = f(iZ))$.

The problem can now be stated as, choose $f(i)$ to minimize

$$\sum_i f(i).t(i) \tag{4.3}$$

subject to

$$\sum_i b(ij).f(i) \geq n(j) \tag{4.4}$$

$$f(i) \geq 0 \tag{4.5}$$

which, for given $t(i)$, $n(j)$, and $b(ij)$, is the standard LP. This reformulated problem allows the simplex algorithm to be used to obtain the optimal $f(i)$. However, there is a slight cost involved in this approach since it merely generates the number of trips that must be made to a centre and does not allocate the goods to any of the centres. What the method does is to choose a set of trips to the various centres such that it is possible at one or the other of the centres visited to buy the required goods at least as many times as required by the consumer. The existence of tied solutions means that in general there will be many possible allocations consistent with the optional trip pattern. This does show, incidentally, why Evans's formulation cannot be utilized in more general cases where it is critical to know exactly which good is bought at which centre (because of price differentials).

The fact that our problem can be cast as an LP means that all of the standard analytical results of that model can be utilized. First, as Evans showed, there is an interesting dual problem which can be stated as, choose $g(j)$ to maximise

$$\sum_j n(j).g(j) \tag{4.6}$$

subject to

$$\sum_j b(ij).g(j) \leq t(i)$$

$$g(j) \qquad \geq 0. \tag{4.7}$$

The $g(j)$ can be interpreted as sums of money per unit of good j. The constraint then states that the total imputed value of all goods sold at a centre must not be larger than the transport cost of visiting the centre. The consumer must maximize the value of his required purchases subject to the value of sold goods nowhere exceeding transport costs.

From standard duality theory we know that non-binding constraints in the primal problem will have zero dual-variable values and vice versa. Hence where the choice of $f(i)$ is such that more purchases of good j could be made than required ($f(i) b(ij) > n(j)$) then the constraint is non-binding and the corresponding $g(j)$ will be zero and no value will be placed on increasing the number of trips required for good j. This could be accomplished without any re-allocation of trips to the various centres. If on the other hand the primal constraint binds, then the value of the $g(j)$ will indicate the extra cost incurred if good j is to be purchased on one more occasion.

A second result of linear programming theory is that the number of (non-zero) activities in the optimal solution cannot be larger than the number of constraints. Hence there will never be more centres used than there are separate goods.

One important feature of our model that has been omitted from discussion is that the solutions for the $f(i)$ must be integral. This restriction was included in Bacon's original algorithm and has recently been noted by Killen (1983) in his discussion of formal programming models, but without showing how to impose the restriction. The extra restriction means that we must re-evaluate the use of linear programming techniques since they do not in general produce integer-valued solutions, and clearly we cannot make 2.62 trips to centre A. Fortunately, it turns out that there are two features of our problem that guarantee that the LP will always have an integer-valued optimum and hence that the simplex method will generate integer-valued solutions without any special precautions or adjustments. The first feature to notice is that the coefficient matrix—the $b(ij)$—has all values at zero or one, while the second feature is that all the values of the constraint vector are integral. These two conditions are sufficient for the solution to the LP to be integer valued. Wagner (1969) discusses this 'integrality' problem. In essence the zero/one nature of the coefficient matrix means that new bases can be formed solely by adding or subtracting rows of the matrix (rather than taking multiples or fractions of rows). The addition or subtraction of the integer-valued constraint vector will maintain new integer values at every step of the algorithm.

It is then clearly straightforward to solve this allocation problem however general the structure of the shopping centres available and whatever the pattern of the consumer's requirements. However, rather than give an example at this stage it is preferable to develop the model one step beyond the Bacon/Evans formulation and to introduce the possibility that there are price differentials between centres. Although this book will not be able to develop such a complete model, the comparatively simple extension of the fixed frequency allocation model to encompass price differentials may be useful in further work on the subject.

(b) A MODEL OF ALLOCATION WITH PRICE DIFFERENTIALS

We have mentioned at various points that it is conceivable that different centres will sell the same good at differing prices. It is well known that for individual items (standardized even by quality and brand) there can be substantial price differentials, but we must go further and argue that representative baskets of items from a particular type of shop may also exhibit price differentials. Indeed, UK experience tends to suggest that there could even be a pattern in the price structure—shops selling a good at larger centres are themselves usually physically larger, have a greater turnover, and may well be cheaper than the same type of shop at a smaller centre. Food supermarkets in town centres are often cheaper than neighbourhood grocery shops. Of course there may be many reasons why this should be so; all we are concerned with is the possibility of price differentials and the development of an analysis that can incorporate such a feature. One fact which is already apparent is the possible sensitivity of the optimum allocation to price differentials. We have seen in the discussion of joint economies that sometimes two (or more) transport costs must be weighed against other transport costs. When the difference is small (as it might well be) then a small purchase price difference between the centres under consideration could affect which is chosen. If it is true that centres with larger ranges of shops do tend to charge lower prices and that prices do matter in determining the allocation of shopping trips then it seems likely that prices will play an important role in modelling the full supply/demand picture, and so we see it as a useful step to generalize even the fixed frequency model to allow for price differentials.

It is clear that once we allow for price differentials we can no longer be indifferent as to which goods are bought on a trip to any given centre and hence we cannot simply attempt to generalize Evans's model. At the same time Bacon's original formulation with the clumsy 'fixed charge' $f(iZ)$ variables is to be avoided. One way to achieve a satisfactory formulation is to define every type of shopping trip by a separate variable—a trip to centre A on which goods 1 and 2 are both purchased is then different from a trip to centre A to buy just good 1. We can illustrate this by a simple two-good two-centre example in which both goods are sold at both centres. The Evans model would have defined two variables:

$f(1)$ — the number of trips to centre 1,

$f(2)$ — the number of trips to centre 2.

The Bacon model would have defined four variables:

$f(1\ 1)$ — the number of trips to centre 1 on which good 1 was purchased,

$f(1\ 2)$ — the number of trips to centre 1 on which good 2 was purchased,

$f(2\ 1)$ — the number of trips to centre 2 on which good 1 was purchased,

$f(2\ 2)$ — the number of trips to centre 2 on which good 2 was purchased.

The new price differential model requires six variables:

$X_1 = {}_1f(1\ 1)$ — the number of trips to centre 1 on which both good 1 and good 2 are purchased,

$X_2 = {}_1f(1\ 0)$ — the number of trips to centre 1 on which just good 1 is purchased,

$X_3 = {}_1f(0\ 1)$ — the number of trips to centre 1 on which just good 2 is purchased,

$X_4 = {}_2f(1\ 1)$ — the number of trips to centre 2 on which both goods are purchased,

$X_5 = {}_2f(1\ 0)$ — the number of trips to centre 2 on which just good 1 is purchased,

$X_6 = {}_2f(0\ 1)$ — the number of trips to centre 2 on which just good 2 is purchased.

The notation is written out in the full (but rather clumsy) form for two goods: ${}_if(m\ n) =$ number of trips to centre i on which those goods, for which m and n are set to unity, are purchased.

Each type of shopping trip is associated with a known cost (travel plus purchase price) so that given the prices and travel costs and requirements we can write the problem in the form, choose the X_i so as to minimize

$$X_1(t_1 + {}_1p_1 + {}_1p_2) + X_2(t_1 + {}_1p_1) + X_3(t_1 + {}_1p_2)$$
$$+ X_4(t_2 + {}_2p_1 + {}_2p_2) + X_5(t_2 + {}_2p_1) + X_6(t_2 + {}_2p_2) \qquad (4.8)$$

subject to

$$X_1 + X_2 + X_4 + X_5 = n(1)$$
$$X_1 + X_3 + X_4 + X_6 = n(2) \qquad (4.9)$$

X_i all positive integer or zero, and where ${}_ip_j$ is the price of good j at centre i and t_i is the cost of one trip to centre i.

The constraints, which impose the condition that the total number of occasions on which good j is purchased must equal the requirement, can now be written as equalities. This formulation is also an LP. Since the coefficient matrix has only zero/one elements and the requirement vector is integral the solution will again be integral without needing to impose any restrictions on the standard simplex algorithm for obtaining the optimum.

Before we go on to a general discussion of the model it is instructive to see how a particular case would be solved. Let the values be:

$$_1p_1 = 7, \quad _2p_1 = 3,$$
$$_1p_2 = 8, \quad _2p_2 = 1,$$
$$t_1 = 8, \quad t_2 = 13,$$
$$n(1) = 2, \quad n(2) = 1.$$

The consumer lives nearer to centre 1 but both goods are cheaper at centre 2. Using the compact form of notation the problem becomes, minimize

$$23X_1 + 15X_2 + 16X_3 + 17X_4 + 16X_5 + 14X_6$$

subject to

$$X_1 + X_2 + X_4 + X_5 = 2$$
$$X_1 + X_3 + X_4 + X_6 = 1$$

X_i all zero or positive integer. We follow Chiang's (1974) account of the revised simplex method of solution. The fact that the constraints are equalities (since there can never be any advantage in buying more of the good than necessary given that it is possible to buy any subset of goods required on a trip) means that in the simplex algorithm it is not necessary to begin by introducing 'slack' variables. The initial tableau is then as in Table 4.4, where X_0 is the level of total costs in the objective function.

The first step is to find a solution basis which requires that we find three variables such that each has a unit coefficient in its own row and zero coefficient in the other two rows (each being unity in a different row). Under these circumstances putting all other variables equal to zero yields a solution for the three variables equal to the right-hand side values of the equations. X_0 is always chosen as the variable to have unit value in the first row (equation). We choose X_2 to enter the second row and X_3 the third. To achieve the zero coefficients in rows 1 and 3 and X_2 in rows 1 and 2 it is necess-

TABLE 4.4
Initial tableau for the linear programme

$$X_0 - 23X_1 - 15X_2 - 16X_3 - 17X_4 - 16X_5 - 14X_6 = 0$$
$$X_1 + X_2 + X_4 + X_5 = 2$$
$$X_1 + X_3 + X_4 + X_6 = 1$$

ary to subtract 15 times row 2 from row 1 and 16 times row 3 from row 1 to yield tableau 1 as in Table 4.5.

It can be seen that $X_0 = 46$, $X_2 = 2$, and $X_3 = 1$ is a possible solution to the model but it is not an optimal solution as indicated by the presence of variables with positive coefficients in the first row. We choose the variable with the largest coefficient (X_4) to enter the basis. The variable whose row has the smallest ratio of right-hand side variable to coefficient of X_4 is chosen to leave the basis (in this case X_3). To keep X_0 and X_2 in the basis we need to subtract row 3 from row 2 (removing X_4) and to subtract 14 times row 3 from row 1. The new tableau becomes as in Table 4.6 and has solution values $X_0 = 32$, $X_2 = 1$, and $X_4 = 1$. Since all elements in the first row have zero or negative coefficients (apart from X_0) the solution is known to be optimal. The cheapest cost allocation is then a value of 32 with one trip to centre 1 to buy good 1 $(X_2 = 1)$ and one trip to centre 2 to buy both goods $(X_4 = 1)$.

The actual operation of the simplex algorithm shows why integer value solutions occur—to obtain the unit values of solution variables in rows 2 and 3 it was necessary merely to subtract the rows which kept the values of the right-hand sides (the solution values) integral. In principle this method can be used for problems of any size, that is, for any (finite) numbers of goods and centres and for any configurations of prices, transport costs, and requirements.

There is one complication which is essential to the analysis of hierarchical structures which we have not yet faced—this is the

TABLE 4.5

First solution tableau to the linear programme

$$X_0 + 8X_1 + 0X_2 + 0X_3 + 14X_4 - X_5 + 2X_6 = 46$$
$$X_1 + X_2 \quad + \quad X_4 + X_5 \quad = 2$$
$$X_1 \quad + X_3 + \quad X_4 \quad + X_6 = 1$$

TABLE 4.6

Second solution tableau to the linear programme

$$X_0 - 6X_1 + 0X_2 - 14X_3 + 0X_4 - X_5 - 12X_6 = 32$$
$$X_2 - X_3 \quad + X_5 - X_6 = 1$$
$$X_1 \quad + X_3 + X_4 \quad + X_6 = 1$$

problem of how to handle the case where certain goods are not sold at a particular centre. There are two possible ways of handling this within the existing framework. The first technique is to use a device employed in linear programming problems which include 'artificial' variables, and to set the price of a good which is not actually sold at a centre at a very large value relative to all other prices and then to treat the model as if the good were sold at that centre. The high price will ensure that the consumer would never attempt to buy the good at that centre in an optimum solution. This can be called the 'big M' method. The second technique is to utilize Evans's feasibility coefficients—the $b(ij)$—to modify the constraint equations. For example, in the two-centre two-good case the general constraints are of the form:

$$X_1.b_{11}.b_{12} + X_2 b_{11} + X_4 b_{21} b_{22} + X_5.b_{21} = n(1)$$
$$X_1.b_{11}.b_{12} + X_3.b_{12} + X_4 b_{21}.b_{22} + X_6.b_{22} = n(2)$$

$$(4.10)$$

so if the $b(ij)$ matrix were changed from

1	1	to	1	0
1	1		1	1

then the constraints in our numerical example would be changed to

$$X_2 + X_4 + X_5 = 2$$
$$X_4 + X_6 = 1$$

At the same time the objective function is modified in the same way so that it becomes, minimize

$$15X_2 + 17X_4 + 16X_5 + 14X_6.$$

This technique of deleting the appropriate elements from the general form of the model is likely to be computationally very much more efficient than the 'big M' approach because it is likely to reduce the number of variables very substantially. In the general case with I centres and J goods we know that the total number of combinations of buying or not buying goods at a centre (which supplies all goods) is

$$\binom{J}{1} + \binom{J}{2} \cdots + \binom{J}{J} = 2^J - 1$$

Hence in the general case where all goods are sold at all centres there are $I(2^J - 1)$ variables in the model. Of these we know that at most J (the number of constraints) will be non-zero in the final solution. For example with four goods and four centres there will be 60 variables in the objective function and only four constraints. If, however, the centres were strictly hierarchical (each one containing one more good than the next smallest) then using the Evans approach to delete non-feasible trips we have 26 possible variables instead. This illustrates both how useful it will be to delete impossible trips from the beginning and how large the problem can be even after such a reduction. Consideration of the nature of the programme tells us that in the optimum there will not be more types of trip than there are goods. Since each type of trip is to just one centre this means that even with price differentials and joint and external economies it will not be necessary to visit more centres than there are goods. Indeed, even if the number of types of trip equals the number of goods the number of centres visited may well be less. This is a very suggestive result in that it gives one reason why many centres in a town may be unused by a given consumer.

Having shown how a solution to the fixed frequency price differential model for an individual consumer can be easily obtained by the use of a linear programming model, we can turn to certain obvious features of the model with price differentials:

(i) As in the model without price differentials, a good need not be purchased at the nearest source of supply. External economies and joint economies, as well as price differentials, can mean that some or all purchases of a good are made further away.

(ii) A good need not be purchased at the cheapest source of supply. The price differential between competing centres must be set against the transport cost differential and this can result in higher-cost centres which are closer to the home being used.

(iii) Even if the nearest centre is also the cheapest it is not automatic that the consumer will purchase the good there on all occasions. If there were an external economy available at a more distant centre then the saving in transport cost could negate the price advantage.

(iv) Goods will often be purchased at more than one source of supply. The existence of external economies for frequently purchased goods at distant centres draws some trade away from the local shops. However, once the external economies are exhausted the good will be purchased nearer home unless the larger centre offers very great price advantages.

EVALUATION OF THE MODELS

The models we have put forward have three key features:

(i) a given good may be sold at different centres at different prices;
(ii) different goods may be purchased by the same consumer at different frequencies;
(iii) different centres may offer different ranges of goods.

We can consider the effects of dropping one or more of these 'degrees of freedom' of the model, starting with the most restrictive case.

1. Equal prices, equal frequencies, and equal availability

If every good is sold at every centre at the same price and is bought at the same frequency then the model can be treated as having a single composite good. All shopping is then done at the nearest centre as in the basic Hotelling model. No centre, then, can attain any advantage over another. Hierarchy has of course been ruled out by assumption.

2. Equal prices and equal availability

In this case all goods would continue to be purchased at the nearest centre even though different numbers of goods would be purchased on different trips. There is neither any price advantage nor a transport cost advantage from possible external economies or joint economies. The relaxation of the equal frequency assumption does not by itself alter the allocation of shopping trips.

3. Equal prices and equal frequency

Differential availability of goods means that for some consumers the nearest shops do not supply all their needs and that more distant shopping centres must be used. Indeed, when the frequencies of purchase of all goods are equal the number of external economies generated will mean that the nearest centre selling all goods will be used for all shopping (in the absence of price differentials which could counteract this effect). Hence a hierarchical structure of supply cannot be sustained. If frequencies and prices are equal then a hierarchy can exist only if we impose Christaller's (1966) assumption that only one good is purchased on any given shopping trip. This shows the critical role played by frequency in explaining the existence of hierarchical shopping structures.

4. Equal frequency and equal availability

This is in effect the many-good generalization of the Hotelling model, with price differentials. In the single-good case trips are allocated just to that centre for which the sum of purchase price plus transport cost is minimized. However, in the many-good case it is not possible at a centre to work with composite goods (with price equal to the sum of the individual prices). Different centres might be cheapest for different goods and if these differentials are large enough then it may be cheaper to pay the extra transport costs involved in visiting several centres rather than doing all the shopping at one centre. Consider the example given in Table 4.7 where the requirement is for 1 unit of each good. We can see that a single multi-purpose trip to *A* would cost 13 and a similar trip to *B* would also cost 13. However, a single trip to *A* to buy good 1 plus a single trip to *B* to buy good 2 will cost 12. The effect of the price differentials is the opposite of the joint economy. It is also possible that the price structure is such that all trade is diverted to the more distant centre (saving a trip to the local centre) even though it is more expensive for one of the goods (but much cheaper for the other). If the price of good 1 at centre *B* falls to 5 then it is cheapest (11 units) to make one trip to *B* for both goods. Thus a form of external economy is generated by the trip to *B* for good 2—it means that the effective cost of adding good 1 is merely 5 while the cost of buying it at centre *A* would be 6 units. However, if this phenomenon occurs it will happen for all units and all shopping will be done at the same centre.

We can see that an effect of equal frequency is that only one centre is used for the purchase of any given good. There is never any reason to use different centres for the different units of the same good. However, in the case where all centres are alike in other respects (in terms of availability) and there is no force tending to produce a hierarchical structure (such as unequal frequency) it is

TABLE 4.7

Data for two-good two-centre case with price differentials

	Centre A	Centre B
Transport cost	2	3
Price of good 1	4	7
Price of good 2	7	3

difficult to see why any systematic price differences should arise, and hence this case is probably not very important.

5. Equal prices

A model with different frequencies and different availabilities but equal prices is, of course, the case considered in the first part of this chapter. The existence of the external economies shows a clear advantage for those shops selling the more widely available goods which locate next to a shop selling a less frequently available good. Not only will they draw trade from consumers who are nearer to them than to any other source of supply, but they will also draw some trade from consumers from further away who, despite having a local source of supply, have to visit the centre because it is the nearest source for the other good. The existence of the differential frequency encourages agglomeration and hierarchical structures. Indeed, it even seems that the size of the shops at centres where there are many other shops might be larger than at centres where there are few (or no) other shops. This in turn might produce the conditions for a stable distribution of differential prices.

It is also clear that, to prevent the existence of external economies at large centres from drawing all trade from smaller centres, it is necessary for the shops which are found in fewest places also to have the lowest frequency of shopping. We can see that one set of conditions which is likely to sustain a hierarchical structure of shops is:

  (i) the possibility of multi-purpose shopping trips;
 (ii) the existence of different frequencies of purchasing different goods;
(iii) a strong tendency for those goods which are purchased most often to be also those which have the smallest market areas and therefore to be most numerous.

6. Equal availability

As with case (4), the existence of differential prices can divert trade away from the nearest source of supply. In addition, the effect of the differential frequency is to allow several centres to be used for the purchase of any one good.

7. Equal frequency

When all frequencies are equal there is no automatic tendency for the consumer to buy all goods on all trips. Differential price advantages can make it worthwhile to buy just subsets of the total range of goods at any centre. There is in general also no tendency to buy at the nearest centre. However, if the largest centres also charge lower prices for all goods (even marginally so) then all shopping will be done at such centres—there being no advantage in using the local shops and a necessity to use the large centres for those shops located only there. Indeed the local shops will only be sustainable if they themselves offer sufficiently large price differentials to overcome the advantage of the 'free trip' provided by the external economies at the larger centre. This price/size correlation seems so implausible that it is unlikely that hierarchical structures can be sustained when the frequency of purchasing all goods is equal.

A final point to note is that, as before, if frequencies are equal then the consumer will make all the purchases of a given good at one centre.

CONCLUSION

The discussion of the fixed frequency models developed and solved in this chapter has highlighted the duality between differential frequency of shopping between goods and the existence of hierarchical structures of shopping centres within a town. Even without relying on the existence of price differentials between centres it has become clear how, once multi-purpose trips are allowed, the existence of a hierarchy of shops is likely to be sustained only if frequencies are different and the most frequently purchased of these goods is that found at most centres. Price differentials are probably likely to reinforce this picture in that the lowest price will probably be at the largest centres. These models show why goods need not be bought at the nearest source of supply (as is assumed in the central place model). We have also seen that only in the case where frequencies differ can a given good be purchased at more than one centre.

The results of this chapter have been obtained for a model in which the order cost element is purely the centre-specific transport cost (which is assumed independent of the number of goods) and, by the light of our results in Chapter 3, this may seem to be unduly restrictive. However, it is obvious that in this fixed frequency model the introduction of good-specific shopping costs would have no effect on the allocation of trips because there would be the same total shopping cost whatever the allocation. Only when frequency is a variable is the magnitude of shopping costs potentially able to affect the choice of location.

This chapter has shown how, for the special case of fixed frequencies of shopping, it is possible to find a solution for the optimal allocation of shopping trips, however complex the urban structure. The solution is not analytical, but the fact that the model can be expressed as a linear programme means that the simplex algorithm, which is known to work, can be used. A very substantial advantage of this restricted model, as we shall see in the next chapter, is that it is fairly easy to generalize the solution, from the case of a single consumer with given transport costs to the various centres (i.e. at a particular point in the town), to the case of all consumers in the town (whatever their set of transport costs). Such a generalization is needed in order to identify the 'market areas' of the various shops in the different centres, which in turn is needed before a full supply/demand analysis could be carried out.

5

THE DETERMINATION OF MARKET AREAS WHEN FREQUENCY IS FIXED

In order to be able to construct a full equilibrium model of urban structure, that is of the number and location of the various types of shop within a town, it is clearly necessary to be able to predict (in the model) the total amount of trade that will be attracted to a given shop. If we continue to make the assumption that bundle size is also fixed, then the problem is essentially to find out which consumers will use the shop in question and for how many trips per unit time period.

There has been a considerable amount of work done on the determination of 'market areas' of shops, but this is all effectively for the one-good case in which none of the complications of the previous chapter can occur. New techniques are required for the many-good case.

With models of this type there are two possible approaches to generating an expression for all the trade going to a given shop. The first approach is a complete household-by-household enumeration of optimum shopping allocations which would allow a summing up over all households that use the centre in question. If we had the distance costs and requirements for each household then, by solving as many linear programming problems as there were households, we could arrive at the total trade for each centre. Even if all households were identical with respect to their requirements they could not be identical with respect to the distance costs. The whole essence of a spatial configuration is that different people live in different places and hence are faced with completely different orderings of the various centres by distance. The solution by complete enumeration would then be immensely costly in computing resources, and for a large town with many centres and goods (where the LP for an individual household had a large number of variables) the task would be immense.

The second approach is to find some way of relating the behaviour of one household to that of others so that in solving the optimum allocations for the one we obtain a solution for a known group of other households. In order to achieve this goal it has been found necessary to introduce three further assumptions:

(i) all households have the same requirements in terms of bundle size and frequency of purchase of each of the goods;
(ii) households are spread evenly and continuously throughout the town (whether this be in one- or two-dimensional space);
(iii) the cost of travelling to and from a given centre is strictly proportional to the distance between the home and the centre.

Before we show how these assumptions allow us to determine with relatively few calculations the market areas of centres it is necessary to examine each of these extra restrictions on our model.

It is obviously restrictive to assume that all households have the same bundle sizes and frequency and indeed, in our analysis in Chapter 2, we placed some stress on identifying those factors which would cause them to vary. We can only defend this assumption by suggesting that for most households the patterns of bundle size and frequency are fairly similar. There is at present no evidence on this and so we can do no more than put it forward as a starting point for the model.

The assumption of uniform and continuous spacing of households is also almost universal in location theory. The purpose of such an assumption is to permit the identification of the location of neighbouring households to any household under study. Clearly, cities and towns are not uniformly packed with households next to each other. However, it is possible to start with the assumption that they are and then remove from the calculated market areas those zones known not to contain households.

The final assumption, that transport costs are strictly proportional to distance, contains several elements:

(i) it assumes that it is possible to travel along a path of shortest route to any given centre;
(ii) it assumes that the same transport mode is available for all households;
(iii) it assumes that costs rise with distance and that there is no fixed cost element to travel;

(iv) it assumes that the relation between cost and distance is the same for all centres.

These assumptions have been generally used in location theory although Lewis (1945) did suggest that marginal and average transport costs might be different, while Zeuthen (1933) and Lerner and Singer (1939) considered transport schedules that were non-linear with respect to distance (but linear with respect to the quantity transported). Some studies have considered cost schedules that are centre-specific (where it costs more per mile to travel to *A* rather than to *B*) irrespective of the consumer's location.

MARKET BOUNDARIES IN THE ONE-GOOD CASE

To illustrate the type of technique that can be used to determine market areas under these conditions we refer to the analysis of Hyson and Hyson (1950), which is the most general study for the one-good case—it is an extension of the work of Fetter (1924), Hotelling (1929) and Schneider (1935).

Let us start by considering a 'linear' town (i.e. where the consumers are spread along a straight line of length L). There are two centres (*A* and *B*) located at L_A and L_B units from the edge of the town (measuring all distances from left to right). The transport costs are $S(A)$ and $S(B)$ for 1 unit of the good bought at *A* or *B* and carried for 1 unit distance. The consumer wishes to purchase 1 unit of the good on one trip (irrespective of cost). The sale prices of the units are $p(A)$ and $p(B)$. The problem is then to identify which households buy from *A* and which from *B*. Figure 5.1 shows the situation.

Clearly all households will buy from *A* for whom

$$p(A) + t(A).S(A) < p(B) + t(B).S(B) \qquad (5.1)$$

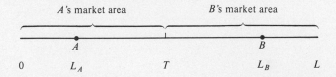

Fig. 5.1 Market areas for the single-good two-centre case in a linear town

where $t(A)$ is the distance of the household to A and $t(B)$ is the distance to B. Hence the boundary between the market areas comes where the inequality sign is replaced by an equality. There are three cases:

(i) there is one boundary, which can come between the centres or outside them;

(ii) there are two boundaries, with both outside the two centres or one between and one outside the centres;

(iii) there is no boundary (one centre attracts all the trade).

The easiest way to see how the various solutions can arise is to construct the purchase cost against distance functions for the two centres and to see where they can intersect. Figure 5.2 shows such a diagram for the case of a single boundary between the centres. The cost curves are made up of the purchase price plus the travel cost, which is proportional to the distance of the household from the centre. The higher the travel cost the steeper the cost function rises from its minimum value. In Figure 5.2 it is cheaper to shop at A for centres living to the left of T and cheaper to shop at B for those living to the right. Two other cases of interest are shown by (a) and (b) in Figure 5.3.

In Figure 5.3(a) it is cheaper to buy from centre A wherever the

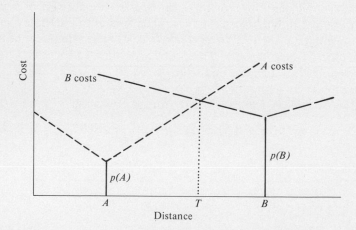

Fig. 5.2 Costs and distances for a one-good two-centre linear town (single-boundary case)

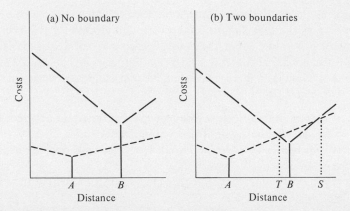

Fig. 5.3 Costs and distances for a one-good two-centre linear town (zero- and two-boundary cases)

consumer lives, and so no trade goes to B; while in Figure 5.3(b) it is cheaper to buy at centre B only for those who live very close to it (between T and S). As the distance rises the much higher transport costs per unit from B make it profitable to switch back to A.

The critical factor that can produce the double boundary is the differential transport cost (which is centre-specific). This possibility is more realistic in studying industrial location theory where the producer may transport the goods to the purchaser and charge for the transport cost. The price charged then enters into the competitive structure and is centre-specific. For the present, we can argue that in the analysis of shopping behaviour the transport mode used is independent of the centre and that prices will be the same everywhere. In such a case there are only two types of solution: either there is a single boundary between the centres or there is no boundary at all. The boundary equation then becomes

$$p(A) + t(A).S = p(B) + t(B).S. \tag{5.2}$$

If the distance between the centres is Γ then we have

$$p(A) + t(A)S = p(B) + \{\Gamma - t(A)\}S \tag{5.3}$$

which gives a solution for $t(A)$. The condition for a boundary to exist is $|p(A) - p(B)| < \Gamma S$, i.e. that the cost of travelling between the centres is greater than the price differential.

The extension to cities spread over the plane (with demand being uniformly spread) gives rise to boundaries which are continuous curves over the two-dimensional space. The boundary is merely a locus of points such that the cost of buying from *A* or from *B* is equal for households located on the boundary. Hyson and Hyson (1950) showed that there were four distinct shapes of boundary in the two-centre case:

(i) if prices and unit transport costs are both equal then the boundary is the straight line equidistant from both centres;

(ii) if unit transport costs are equal but prices are not equal then the boundary is a hyperbola;

(iii) if prices are equal but unit transport costs are unequal then the boundary is circular;

(iv) if both prices and unit transport costs are unequal then the boundary is a hypercircle ('Descartes' oval').

In the one-good case we will continue to argue that transport costs are equal and so only cases (i) and (ii) apply. Figure 5.4 shows a boundary when prices are unequal.

The technique of deriving the boundary is as follows. Let the *x* axis be that line passing through the centres *A* and *B* and let the *y* axis be a line orthogonal to it and passing midway between *A* and *B*. Let the distances to an arbitrary point on the boundary be *t* and *u*. Then, if the prices at the two centres are *p* and *q* (with *q* greater than *p* in our diagram):

$$p + t.s = q + u.s \tag{5.4}$$

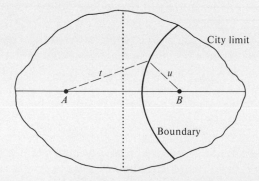

Fig. 5.4 Market areas for single-good two-centre case in a two-dimensional town

where s is the transport cost per unit distance. If the centres are $2a$ units apart ($\Gamma = 2a$) then

$$t = \sqrt{\{(x+a)^2 + y^2\}} \tag{5.5}$$

$$u = \sqrt{\{(x-a)^2 + y^2\}}. \tag{5.6}$$

Substituting equation (5.5) and equation (5.6) into equation (5.4) and solving we obtain an equation of the form

$$x^2/c^2 - y^2/d^2 = 1 \tag{5.7}$$

where

$$c = (q-p)/2s \tag{5.8}$$

$$d = a^2 - c^2. \tag{5.9}$$

Equation (5.7) is a hyperbola in the general case.

So far the discussion has concentrated on identifying the boundaries and market areas for the two-centre case. The many-centre case is essentially similar but it is useful to discuss it at this stage because of the complications which arise in analysing the many-centre many-good case. The technique which is used to delimit market areas when there are (say) three centres is to take the three pairwise comparisons. First, we can establish which zone prefers A to B, then which prefers B to C, and finally, which prefers C to A. Figure 5.5 shows the case when prices are the same at all three centres. When prices are equal at a pair of centres then we know that the boundary is a straight line equidistant from both centres. Hence, comparing A and B we see that every household above the line bb' prefers B to A and below the line prefers A to B. As between A and C the points to the left of aa' prefer A to C, while households above cc' prefer B to C. Clearly there can be no contradictions in preferences—a household cannot prefer A to B, B to C and yet prefer C to A. This implies that the three pairwise preferred boundaries must meet in a point at O. The market areas are then determined: A attracts all households lying nearer to it than the boundary aOb etc.

When prices are unequal then the boundaries are determined by the intersection of three hyperbolic arcs (which again must meet in a point to yield consistent preferences) unless the differentials are so great that one or two centres can never compete with the third centre and attract no customers.

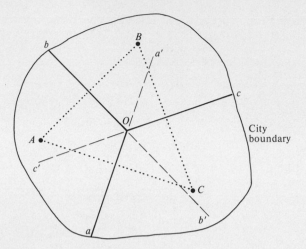

Fig. 5.5 Market areas for single-good three-centre case with equal prices in a two-dimensional city

If we desired to obtain an expression for the amount of trade going to a particular centre it would be necessary to determine the area enclosed by the intersecting boundaries. If the equation of the limits of the city were known (for example a circle of known radius) then this problem could be solved using standard integration techniques over two-dimensional regions with boundaries given by the techniques described here.

MARKET BOUNDARIES IN THE MANY-GOOD CASE

The analysis of the one-good case cannot be simply carried over to the many-good case. In the single-good case it was shown how consumers use the centre for which the sum of price plus transport cost is least. Our discussion of the many-good case in Chapter 4 showed that on occasions households shop where neither price nor transport cost (nor their sum) is lowest. This phenomenon, it was shown, arises because of the existence of 'external' and 'joint' economies. What is needed is a method of determining the set of all households for whom the solution to the allocation problem is the same.

(a) LINEAR CITY CASE

We begin with a simple two-good two-centre linear city model. The city is L units in length and the centres are located at L_A and L_B units from the left-hand side of the city. Both centres sell both goods but at different prices. The objective function for a consumer living at the left-hand edge of the city is then, minimize

$$(_A p_1 + t.L_A)X_2 + (_A p_2 + t.L_A)X_3 + (_A p_1 + _A p_2 + tL_A)X_1 +$$
$$(_B p_1 + t.L_B)X_5 + (_B p_2 + t.L_B)X_6 + (_B p_1 + _B p_2 + tL_B)X_4 \quad (5.10)$$

subject to

$$X_1 + X_2 + X_4 + X_5 = n_1$$
$$X_1 + X_3 + X_4 + X_6 = n_2 \quad (5.11)$$

where (following the notation in Chapter 4)

$X_1 = $ trips to A to buy both goods,

$X_2 = $ trips to A to buy good 1 etc.,

$n_j = $ requirements for good j.

This problem can be solved as indicated in Chapter 4 for known values of the prices and transport cost and requirements. The problem is to solve a similar problem for all households without doing an enormous number of calculations. The experience of the single-good case where neighbouring households (on one side of the boundary) all have the same solution suggests that we could use a similar approach. Consider a household living an arbitrary D units from the left-hand edge but to the right of centre $A(D \le L_A)$. For such a household the constraints remain the same as equation (5.11) but the objective function becomes, minimize

$$(_A p_1 + t[L_A - D])X_2 + (_A p_2 + t[L_A - D])X_3$$
$$+ (_A p_1 + _A p_2 + t[L_A - D])X_1 + (_B p_1 + t[L_B - D])X_5$$
$$+ (_B p_2 + t[L_B - D])X_6 + (_B p_1 + _B p_2 + t[L_B - D])X_4. \quad (5.12)$$

The problem is then to find the solutions for all values of D. This in fact is a standard parametric linear programme of the form:

minimize

$$c'y + Dd'y \quad (5.13)$$

subject to

$$Ay = b \qquad (5.14)$$

for

$$0 \leq D \leq K. \qquad (5.15)$$

Such problems are discussed in standard books on LP techniques, such as Gass (1969), and are solved by a method introduced by Saaty and Gass (1954). We can anticipate our discussion of the technique of solutions to remark that the method finds the set of values of D at which the solution changes (call these D_1, D_2, etc.). Between successive switch points (called 'characteristic' values) the solution remains the same for all values of D. Hence if we can identify the finite set of D_i at which the solutions change we can give the solutions for all the (infinite) points on the line.

The programme as described in equation (5.12) is generally valid for any household living to the left of A but must be altered for households living between A and B to, minimize

$$
\begin{aligned}
&({}_Ap_1 + t[D-L_A])X_2 + ({}_Ap_2 + t[D-L_A])X_3 \\
&+ ({}_Ap_1 + {}_Ap_2 + t[D-L_A]X_1 + ({}_Bp_1 + t[L_B-D])X_5 \\
&+ ({}_Bp_2 + t[L_B-D])X_6 + ({}_Bp_1 + {}_Bp_2 + t[L_B-D])X_4 \qquad (5.16)
\end{aligned}
$$

with the same constraints and for $L_A \leq D \leq L_B$. Finally, for households living to the right of B the programme is, minimize

$$
\begin{aligned}
&({}_Ap_1 + t[D-L_A])X_2 + ({}_Ap_2 + t[D-L_A])X_3 \\
&+ ({}_Ap_1 + {}_Ap_2 + t[D-L_A])X_1 + ({}_Bp_1 + t[D-L_B])X_5 \\
&+ ({}_Bp_2 + t[D-L_B])X_6 + ({}_Bp_1 + {}_Bp_2 + t[D-L_B])X_4 \qquad (5.17)
\end{aligned}
$$

for $L_B \leq D \leq L$. Hence for the two-centre case we have shown that we can obtain the set of all solutions and their boundaries by solving three parametric programmes.

We show how the technique is used by taking the specific values:

$$
\begin{array}{lll}
{}_Ap_1 = 7, & {}_Ap_2 = 8, & \\
{}_Bp_1 = 3, & {}_Bp_2 = 1, & \\
L_A = 8, & L_B = 13, & L = 16, \\
n_1 = 2, & n_2 = 1, & t = 1.
\end{array}
$$

The parametric programme for all consumers living to the left of centre A is then, minimize

$$(23-D)X_1+(15-D)X_2+(16-D)X_3+(17-D)X_4$$
$$+(16-D)X_5+(14-D)X_6 \tag{5.18}$$

subject to

$$X_1+X_2+X_4+X_5=2$$
$$X_1+X_3+X_4+X_6=1 \tag{5.19}$$

all X_i integer or zero, $0\leq D\leq 8$.

If we followed the same manipulations as in Chapter 4 (i.e. making the same row additions and subtractions) the last tableau would now have as its first row

$$X_0-(6-D)X_1+DX_2-(14-D)X_3+DX_4-(1-D)X_5$$
$$-(12-D)X_6=32 \tag{5.20}$$

and rows 2 and 3 would be as before (since D does not enter these rows). Equation (5.20), however, cannot serve as a final basis because the two proposed solution variables (X_2 and X_4) have non-zero coefficients (if $D\neq0$). Hence to obtain a solution for all D we must subtract D times row 2 and D times row 3 to yield as a final tableau that shown in Table 5.1.

TABLE 5.1
Final tableau for parametric programme 1

X_0	X_1	X_2	X_3	X_4	X_5	X_6	Constant
1	-6	0	$-(14-D)$	0	-5	$-(12-D)$	$32-2D$
0	0	1	-1	0	1	-1	1
0	1	0	1	1	0	0	1

This has as its basis:

$$X_0=32-2D$$
$$X_2=1$$
$$X_4=1 \tag{5.21}$$

all other X_i zero. From the coefficients of the first row we can obtain the conditions under which this basis is optimal. For optimality all coefficients of non-basic variables must be negative and we can see that this is true provided that

$$14-D>0$$
and $$12-D>0. \tag{5.22}$$

Hence, provided D is less than 12, the solution indicated by equation (5.21) is optimal. Since the city stretches for only 8 units to the left of centre A we see that a solution with $X_2 = 1$, $X_4 = 1$ is optimal for all customers living to the left of centre A. Of course the value of the solution (in terms of total costs) changes with D, but all customers still make one trip to centre A for good 1 and one trip to centre B on which both goods are bought.

We next consider the programme for those households living between A and B which has objective function, minimize

$$(7 + D)X_1 + (D - 1)X_2 + DX_3 + (17 - D)X_4 + (16 - D)X_5$$
$$+ (14 - D)X_6 \qquad (5.23)$$

where $8 \leq D \leq 13$. From the previous model we know that at $D = 8$ the optimal solution is $X_2 = 1$ and $X_4 = 1$, so we try this for our initial basis. We go from tableau 1 (Table 5.2) to tableau 2 (Table 5.3) by adding $(D - 1)$ times row 2 and $(18 - 2D)$ times row 3 to row 1 and subtracting row 3 from row 2. All the coefficients in the first row are negative (for values of D in the critical range) if

$$2D < 17 \qquad (5.24)$$

since the other coefficients are positive only for values of D outside the range specified. Hence for all households between $D = 8$ and $D = 8.5$ the solution continues to be $X_2 = 1$ and $X_4 = 1$ (with value of solution equal to 16). At $D = 8.5$ it is clear that variable X_5 must

TABLE 5.2
Initial tableau for household between centres

X_0	X_1	X_2	X_3	X_4	X_5	X_6	Constant
1	$-(7+D)$	$-(D-1)$	$-D$	$-(17-D)$	$-(16-D)$	$-(14-D)$	0
0	1	1	0	1	1	0	2
0	1	0	1	1	0	1	1

TABLE 5.3
Second tableau for household between centres

X_0	X_1	X_2	X_3	X_4	X_5	X_6	Constant
1	$(10-2D)$	0	$(18-3D)$	0	$(2D-17)$	$(4-D)$	16
0	0	1	-1	0	1	-1	1
0	1	0	1	1	0	1	1

enter the solution and row 2 (variable X_2) must be removed (in accordance with the usual simplex criteria). This can be achieved simply by subtracting $(2D-17)$ times row 2 from row 1 to yield tableau 3 (Table 5.4). This basis has a solution

$$X_0 = 33 - 2D$$
$$X_5 = 1 \qquad\qquad (5.25)$$
$$X_4 = 1$$

which is optimal (in the appropriate region) if

$$2D > 17. \qquad\qquad (5.26)$$

The inequality is of course the left-hand boundary at 8.5 which marks the beginning of the zone in which consumers make one trip to centre B for both goods ($X_4 = 1$) and one trip to centre B for just good 1 ($X_5 = 1$). There is then just the single characteristic value at 8.5 in the region between centres. Although the model indicates that there is a boundary at $D = 13$ this is the point where the objective function changes again so that we cannot tell what happens beyond this value from the programme for the between-centre households.

TABLE 5.4
Third tableau for household between centres

X_0	X_1	X_2	X_3	X_4	X_5	X_6	Constant
1	$(10-2D)$	$(17-2D)$	$(1-D)$	0	0	$(D-13)$	$33-2D$
0	0	1	-1	0	1	-1	1
0	1	0	1	1	0	1	1

A third application of this technique using the programme (5.17) for consumers to the right of centre B and taking $X_4 = 1$ and $X_5 = 1$ as an initial allocation reveals that this is optimal for the whole range to the right of centre B and that the value of the programme is $(2D-19)$. The complete solution is then:

$$0 \le D \le 8 \quad X_2 = 1,\ X_4 = 1,\ X_0 = 32 - 2D$$
$$8 \le D \le 8.5 \quad X_2 = 1,\ X_4 = 1,\ X_0 = 16$$
$$8.5 \le D \le 13 \quad X_4 = 1,\ X_5 = 1,\ X_0 = 33 - 2D$$
$$13 \le D \le 16 \quad X_4 = 1,\ X_5 = 1,\ X_0 = 2D - 19.$$

This illustration of the use of parametric programming shows how easy it is to use and how economically the complete set of solutions to the problem can be generated. We plot the solution values and distance in Figure 5.6. The costs for the consumers do not necessarily change with distance, as the section between 8 and 8.5 shows (increasing distance to A is balanced by the shorter trip to B).

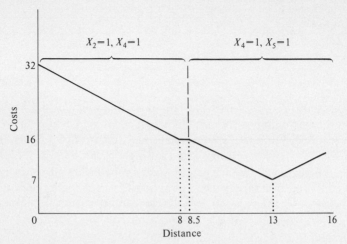

Fig. 5.6 Value of optimal solution in a two-good two-centre case with fixed frequencies in a linear town

The market areas for the shops at the two centres can be immediately read off from the solutions:

  (i) shop 1 at centre A takes 1 unit of trade from all the city to the left of A and from the city up to 0.5 units to the right of A (8.5 units in total);
 (ii) shop 2 at centre A sells nothing;
(iii) shop 1 at centre B sells 1 unit to the whole city and 1 further unit to all consumers living to the right of the point 0.5 units to the right of A (23.5 units in total);
 (iv) shop 2 at centre B sells 1 unit to the whole city (16 units in total).

The graphs of demand against distance (equivalent to the so-called 'demand cones' of classical location theory) are shown in Figure 5.7. Even in the special case of demand inelasticity that we have been considering so far we see that there is a tendency for demand to fall off with distance. The reason for the shift in demand is that at a

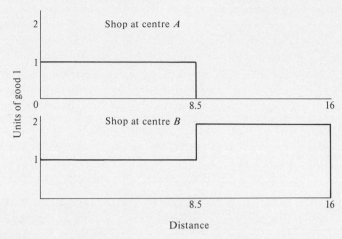

Fig. 5.7 Demand cones for good 1 in a two-good two-centre case with fixed frequencies in a linear town

certain point the advantages of buying the one odd unit at centre A because of low transport costs in its neighbourhood is overcome by the cheapness of good 1 at centre B. The model predicts sharp boundaries occurring between centres (if they occur at all).

We next consider the generalization of the two-centre linear city model to the many-good case. As we have shown in Chapter 4, this can be formulated as a linear programme with a larger number of variables. It is of some interest to consider the maximum number of boundaries there can be. We begin with two goods purchased at frequencies $n(1)$ and $n(2)$, $(n(1) \geq n(2))$. There are $n(1) - n(2)$ trips that must be made solely for good 1, and in the case of two centres there is at most one boundary dividing the market areas between the two centres (if the Hyson and Hyson condition is not met, all this demand goes to one or other centre). We next consider the $n(2)$ occasions on which both goods are required. If both are purchased at the same centre there is at most one boundary dividing the centres. However, this boundary must in general be in a different place from that for good 1 since it involves purchasing two goods. More generally, there can be two boundaries. To the left of the area between the two centres both goods are bought at A, in the middle, one good is bought at each centre, and to the right both are bought at B. The following values yield this solution when the requirement is for 1 unit of each good:

$$_A p_1 = 3, \quad _A p_2 = 6,$$
$$_B p_1 = 7, \quad _B p_2 = 3,$$

the distance between the centres being 5 units. For the purchase of the single unit of good 1 the boundary is at 4.5 units to the right of A. For the 1 unit of good 1 and 1 of good 2 the boundaries are:

(i) to the left of α (2 units to the right of A) buy both goods at A;
(ii) between α and β (4 units to the right of A) buy good 1 at centre A and good 2 at centre B;
(iii) to the right of β buy both goods on a single trip to centre B.

Finally, we need to note that if it is optimal to buy good 1 at A and good 2 at B it will never be optimal to buy good 1 at B and good 2 at A. Since each centre is visited once in both cases the transport cost element is the same in both, and since the given combination of prices is clearly invariant with respect to distance it follows that the two types of allocation cannot both be optimal. Hence we see that for two goods purchased at the same frequency there are at most two boundaries (three regions). Hence for the two-good case with different frequencies the maximum number of boundaries is three, which gives a maximum number of solution regions of four. Figure 5.8 gives the solution regions for the revised example.

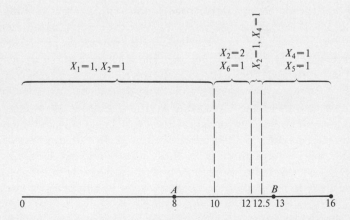

Fig. 5.8 Solution regions for a revised two-good two-centre case with fixed frequencies in a linear town

We turn next to the three-good model. In the general case all three frequencies are different. There must be $n(1) - n(2)$ trips just for good 1 and this gives one boundary. There must be $n(2) - n(3)$ occasions on which goods 1 and 2 are also purchased and there will, as in the previous case, be at most two boundaries for these trips. Finally there are $n(3)$ occasions on which all three goods must be purchased and there can at most be three boundaries for such a case. As we move from left to right, once we pass a point where a good stops being allocated to A and is allocated to B there cannot be a further point to the right at which it is re-allocated to A. Hence there can be at most three switching points. There are thus at most six boundaries (seven market areas) for distinct allocations in the three-good case.

In the general two-centre case where all frequencies are distinct there are, by extension of the preceding argument, $\sum_1^J j (= J(J+1)/2)$ boundaries at most. If the frequencies are bunched (i.e. several goods having the same frequency) then the maximum number of boundaries drops. We can see that even in the case of many goods in the two-centre case the three parametric linear programmes that are required are not likely to generate a very great number of distinct boundaries and solution regions.

We next consider the many-centre case, starting with one good. Let the centres be labelled from left to right $A, B,$ and C. There can be at most one boundary between A and B and another between B and C (or else just a single boundary somewhere between A and C when B is never used). Any attempt to locate a third boundary between centres A and C would produce a contradiction. Hence there are at most two boundaries and three regions. With two goods there can be at most four boundaries with two between each pair of centres. This argument can be generalized and it appears that in the I-centre J-good case there are at most $(I-1)(J+1)/2$ boundaries.

The parametric programme for the many-centre case for the linear city is relatively simple to operate because it can be formulated in a special way with respect to the distance parameter. For households lying in any given section of the city (i.e. between a given pair of centres) the distances to all centres can be related to the single parameter. Consider the three-centre case where the distance between the first pair of centres is $\Gamma(1)$ and that between the next pair is $\Gamma(2)$. Then for all points lying between A and B the distances are:

$$\text{distance to } A = D$$
$$\text{distance to } B = \Gamma(1) - D$$
$$\text{distance to } C = \Gamma(1) + \Gamma(2) - D$$

(D is now measured as a distance from the left-hand-space edge of the city). Hence, however many centres and goods there are, a single parametric programme can be used to solve the allocation for all households in a given sector.

(b) TWO-DIMENSIONAL CITY CASE

In the case of a two-dimensional city where consumers are spread evenly over the plane (or a sub-region of the plane) matters are not so simple because we cannot index the set of distances to the centres for a group of consumers by a single parameter. Indeed, as equations (5.5) and (5.6) show, the general expression for the distances to a pair of centres from an arbitrary point is given by a pair of non-linear functions using the axes of the city as the coordinates. Entering this non-linear structure into our linear programme would make for a very awkward optimization and it is easier to take an alternative approach. Let us define D_1 and D_2 as the distances from an arbitrary point to centres 1 and 2. We can then consider the parametric linear programme in which both distances can be varied. This should yield sets of D_1 and D_2 which form boundaries for solutions, and such sets (if linked together by a known equation) can then be translated into a boundary in the city space. An example will help to clarify the procedure and so we begin with a two-good centre model which has values:

$$_A p_1 = 7, \quad _A p_2 = 8,$$
$$_B p_1 = 3, \quad _B p_2 = 1,$$
$$n(1) = 2, \ n(1) = 1, \ t = 1.$$

The programme for an arbitrary consumer is then, minimize

$$(15 + D_1)X_1 + (7 + D_1)X_2 + (8 + D_1)X_3 + (4 + D_2)X_4 + (3 + D_2)X_5 +$$
$$(1 + D_2)X_6 \tag{5.27}$$

subject to

$$X_1 + X_2 + X_4 + X_5 = 2$$
$$X_1 + X_3 + X_4 + X_6 = 1$$

with X_i zero or positive integer, and for all D_i in the feasible range. As a starting point we take $D_1 = D_2 = 0$ (although no consumer actually will have such values) and the final tableau, starting with an initial basis of X_2 and X_4, is as given in Table 5.5. The final basis

TABLE 5.5
Final tableau for $D_1 = D_2 = 0$

X_0	$-11X_1$	$-4X_2$	$-7X_3$	$+0X_3$	$+0X_5$	$+0X_6$	$=7$
		X_2	$-X_3$		$+X_5$	$-X_6$	$=1$
	X_1		$+X_3$	$+X_4$		$+X_6$	$=1$

has $X_5 = 1$ and $X_4 = 1$ with a value of 7. The introduction of two parameters into the objective function follows the 'double description' method of Gass and Saaty (1955). If we increase the costs of all trips to centre 1 by D_1 and the trips to centre 2 by D_2 we alter the original tableau and if we follow exactly the same row manipulations as before we arrive at the following first row (the second and third being unchanged):

$$X_0 - (11 + D_1)X_1 - (4 + D_1)X_2 - (7 + D_1)X_3 - D_2 X_4 - D_2 X_5$$
$$- D_2 X_6 = 7. \tag{5.28}$$

This is no longer optimal but can be made so by adding D_2 times row 2 and D_2 times row 3 to yield

$$X_0 - (11 + D_1 - D_2)X_1 - (4 + D_1 - D_2)X_2 - (7 + D_1)X_3 + 0X_4 + 0X_5$$
$$- D_2 X_6 = 7 + 2D_2. \tag{5.29}$$

All coefficients remain negative and hence the solution remains optimal provided that

$$11 + D_1 - D_2 > 0$$
$$4 + D_1 - D_2 > 0$$
$$7 + D_1 > 0 \tag{5.30}$$
$$D_2 > 0.$$

The last two inequalities are of no interest to our particular problem since they are required in order to keep distances positive.

The second inequality implies the first and so there is a solution boundary at $4 + D_1 = D_2$. We plot these boundaries in Figure 5.9 which is in (D_1, D_2) space, and we can see that the boundary is a straight line cutting off the open region **A**. Hence for all values of D_1 and D_2 that are positive and which obey the restriction $4 + D_1 > D_2$ the optimum allocation is $X_4 = 1$, $X_5 = 1$ (i.e. one trip to B to buy both goods and one trip to B to buy just good 1).

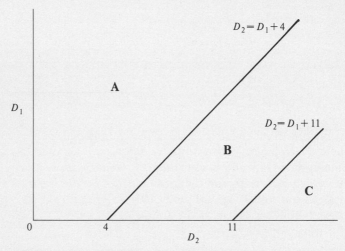

Fig. 5.9 Solution regions for two-good two-centre case with fixed frequencies in a two-dimensional town

It follows that on all boundaries of region **A** there is a change of basis. Since two of the boundaries are economically uninteresting we can turn to the third boundary. The simplex algorithm indicates that X_2 enters the solution and X_5 leaves. To obtain a new basis with X_2 in row 2 and X_4 in row 3 we need to add $(4 + D_1 - D_2)$ times row 2 to row 1 to yield

$$X_0 - (11 + D_1 - D_2)X_1 + 0X_2 - (11 + 2D_1 - D_2)X_3 + 0X_4$$
$$+ (4 + D_1 - D_2)X_5 - (4 + D_1)X_6 = 11 + D_1 + D_2 \qquad (5.31)$$

with rows 2 and 3 as before (but with basis $X_2 = 1$, $X_4 = 1$). This new basis is optimal provided that

$$11 + D_1 - D_2 > 0$$
$$11 + 2D_1 - D_2 > 0$$
$$\qquad (5.32)$$

$$4 + D_1 - D_2 < 0$$
$$4 + D_1 > 0$$

For positive values the first constraint implies the second and the fourth is automatically satisfied. The third constraint is merely the boundary of **A** looked at from the right and indicates where the solution changes back to that established for region **A**. The new constraint is the first which indicates that on the line $11 + D_1 = D_2$ the solution changes again. Hence the open region **B** (bounded by the first and third constraints) gives all values for D_1 and D_2 for which a solution $X_2 = 1$, $X_4 = 1$ is optimal. We can move to the right-hand boundary of **B** to find the next solution region. The simplex indicates that X_1 enters the basis and X_4 must be removed. From equation (5.31) we can see that $(11 + D_1 - D_2)$ times row 3 must be added to row 1 and that no other changes are needed. The new row 1 is

$$X_0 + 0X_1 + 0X_2 - D_1X_3 + (11 + D_1 - D_2)X_4 + (4 + D_1 - D_2)X_5$$
$$+ (7 - D_2)X_6 = 22 + 2D_1. \tag{5.33}$$

The basis is now $X_1 = 1$, $X_2 = 1$ (i.e. one trip to centre A to buy both goods and one trip to A to buy good 1). This solution remains optimal provided that

$$D_1 > 0$$
$$(11 + D_1 - D_2) < 0$$
$$(4 + D_1 - D_2) < 0 \tag{5.34}$$
$$D_2 - 7 > 0.$$

The second inequality implies the third and is merely the boundary of **B** looked at from the right. The second constraint also implies the fourth for positive values. Hence region **C** is open and is bounded by the axis and the second constraint. This also indicates that there are no more solution regions—whatever the values of D_1 and D_2 there are at most the three regions:

region **A**	$D_1 > 0$	
	$D_2 > 0$	$X_4 = 1, X_5 = 1$
	$D_2 < D_1 + 4$	
region **B**	$D_1 > 0$	
	$D_2 > D_1 + 4$	$X_2 = 1, X_4 = 1$
	$D_2 < D_1 + 11$	

region **C** $\quad\quad$ $D_1 > 0$
$\quad\quad\quad\quad\quad\quad$ $D_2 > D_1 + 11$ $\quad\quad$ $X_1 = 1, X_2 = 1$

We see that one feasible combination ($X_1 = 1$, $X_5 = 1$) is never optimal.

Since the phase diagram constructed in Figure 5.9 gives the solutions for all possible distances from the centres we can now consider transferring the solution boundaries onto the map of the city. By considering the location of the two centres (specifically the distance between them) we can rule out regions in D space that cannot exist in the city and hence are not of interest. Let us consider the case where the centres are Γ units apart. This places two restrictions on the D_i. First,

$$D_1 + D_2 \geq \Gamma. \tag{5.35}$$

This equation says that the sum of the (straight-line) distances from any point to the two centres must be greater than or equal to the distance between the two centres (equality occurring for points on the line) joining the two centres). Second,

$$|D_2 - D_1| \leq \Gamma. \tag{5.36}$$

This equation says that the difference in distances between the more distant and the nearer centre can never be greater than the distance between the two centres. These three inequalities (since the second is in effect two) limit the region of feasible solutions as shown in Figure 5.10, where we take a value of $\Gamma = 5$ (which corresponds to the case studied in Chapter 4). The three extra inequalities are indicated by the dashed lines. Outside these lines there are no points which can have the given combinations of the D_i for centres 5 units apart. The solution regions now become:

region **A$_1$** $\quad\quad$ $D_1 + D_2 \geq 5$
$\quad\quad\quad\quad\quad\quad$ $|D_2 - D_1| \leq 5$ $\quad\quad$ $X_4 = 1$
$\quad\quad\quad\quad\quad\quad$ $D_2 \leq 4 + D_1$ $\quad\quad$ $X_5 = 1$

region **B$_1$** $\quad\quad$ $D_1 + D_2 \geq 5$
$\quad\quad\quad\quad\quad\quad$ $|D_2 - D_1| \leq 5$ $\quad\quad$ $X_2 = 1$
$\quad\quad\quad\quad\quad\quad$ $D_2 \geq 4 + D_1$ $\quad\quad$ $X_4 = 1$

The other sub-regions of **A**(**A$_2$** and **A$_3$**) and of **B**(**B$_2$** and **B$_3$**) are infeasible and so is the whole of region **C**. For cities with centres only 5 units apart the solution in **C**($X_1 = 1$, $X_2 = 1$) is never optimal.

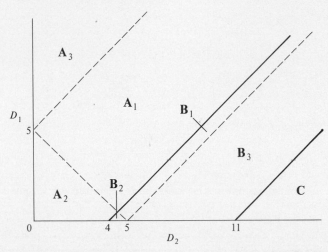

Fig. 5.10 Feasible solution regions with $\Gamma = 5$ for the two-good two-centre fixed frequency case

However, only the boundary between A_1 and B_1 indicates a change in solution since the other boundaries are concerned merely with the existence of the points.

We can now examine the single boundary for the $\Gamma = 5$ case. This boundary has the property that on it $D_2 = 4 + D_1$ and so we are looking for a line such that the difference in distances is a constant. However, this is exactly the form of the boundary in the Hyson and Hyson (1950) case where transport costs per unit from the two centres are equal, and so we know that the boundary must be hyperbolic and must pass through the line joining the two centres at a distance of ½ from centre A (as can be seen from the intersection of the solution boundary with the line $D_1 + D_2 = \Gamma$). This simple extension of the solution space found for the one-good model is shown in Figure 5.11. The boundary is in fact for a single good being switched from A to B (over the whole region one trip is made to centre B to buy both goods), and corresponds to that for a good with a price differential of 4. The equation of the boundary can then easily be obtained from equation (5.7).

The flexibility of solving for the general case at all distances and then imposing the constraints relating to the exact location of the centres can be seen if we now consider the case of two centres a different number of units apart. Let us suppose that $\Gamma = 12$. All we

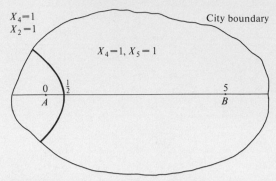

Fig. 5.11 Solution regions in a two-dimensional city for the two-good two-centre case (with $\Gamma = 5$)

need to do is to modify the boundary constraints to yield Figure 5.12. The boundaries from the parametric programme remain in the same places but the feasibility boundaries are altered and there is now a third solution region C_1 given by the equation $D_2 = 11 + D_1$. Translating this onto our map of the city we obtain Figure 5.13. We can see that the same boundary ($D_2 = 4 + D_1$) gives a different intersection on the line joining the centres as the distance between the

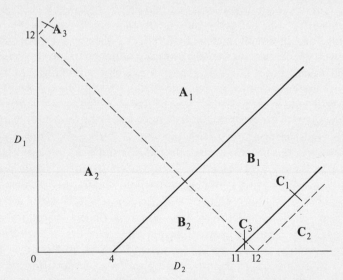

Fig. 5.12 Feasible solution regions with $\Gamma = 12$ in the two-good two-centre fixed frequency case

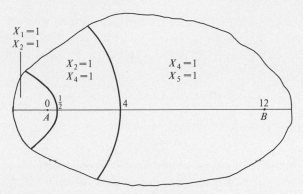

Fig. 5.13 Solution regions in a two-dimensional city for the two-good two-centre case (with $\Gamma = 12$)

centres increases. One boundary holds constant the purchase of 1 unit of good 1 at centre A ($X_2 = 1$) and switches from a trip for both goods to A ($X_1 = 1$) to a trip for both to B ($X_4 = 1$). The other boundary holds constant the purchase of both goods at B and switches from the purchase of 1 unit of good 1 at A ($X_2 = 1$) to 1 unit of good 1 at B ($X_5 = 1$). Both arcs are seen to be hyperbolic from the form of the boundary equations in D space.

However, the discussion of the one-dimensional case reveals two features for the two-dimensional case:

(i) There will be at least as many boundary arcs in the two-dimensional case as there are points in the one-dimensional case, since each point on the line joining the two centres corresponds to an arc;

(ii) Not all arcs are hyperbolic or straight lines (the degenerate case when there are no price differentials). Some switches can be made without involving transport costs to both centres and this results in circular arcs, which also implies that boundaries can intersect even in the two-centre case.

The example in the one-dimensional case made it clear that there are two types of boundary. First, where a trip for a good is switched from centre A to centre B so that we have

$$_1p_A + t_A = {_1p_B} + t_B. \tag{5.37}$$

This yields an equation in which the difference in distances (transport costs) is a constant. If the prices are different this yields a hyperbolic arc, while if prices are equal the arc becomes a straight line. Second, there is the case where a trip to A to buy both goods is replaced by a trip to A for good 1 and a trip to B for good 2. The boundary equation is then

$$t_A + {}_1p_A + {}_2p_A = t_A + {}_1p_A + t_B + {}_2p_B \qquad (5.38)$$

or

$$_2p_A = t_B + {}_2p_B. \qquad (5.39)$$

The boundary is then a constant distance from centre 2 and is thus a circle. We can illustrate with our revised values by letting

$$_1p_A = 3, \ {}_1p_B = 7,$$
$$_2p_A = 6, \ {}_2p_B = 3.$$

The initial row 1 becomes

$$X_0 - (9 + D_1)X_1 - (3 + D_1)X_2 - (6 + D_1)X_3 - (10 + D_2)X_4$$
$$- (7 + D_2)X_5 - (3 + D_2)X_6 = 0. \qquad (5.40)$$

Following the standard parametric programming approach we obtain the following solution regions:

region **A**
$$\left. \begin{array}{r} D_1 > 0 \\ (1 + D_2 - D_1) > 0 \\ (4 + D_2 - D_1) > 0 \\ 3 - D_2 < 0 \end{array} \right\} \quad X_2 = 1, \ X_1 = 1$$

region **B**
$$\left. \begin{array}{r} 3 - D_2 > 0 \\ 3 + D_1 - D_2 > 0 \\ 4 - D_1 > 0 \\ 4 + D_2 - D_1 > 0 \end{array} \right\} \quad X_2 = 2, \ X_6 = 1$$

region **C**
$$\left. \begin{array}{r} D_1 - D_2 - 1 > 0 \\ 2D_1 - D_2 - 1 > 0 \\ 4 + D_2 - D_1 > 0 \\ 4 - D_1 < 0 \end{array} \right\} \quad X_2 = 1, \ X_4 = 1$$

region **D**
$$\left. \begin{array}{r} D_1 - D_2 - 1 > 0 \\ D_1 - D_2 - 4 > 0 \\ 3D_1 - 2D_2 - 5 > 0 \\ D_2 > 0 \end{array} \right\} \quad X_4 = 1, \ X_5 = 1.$$

These regions are plotted in Figure 5.14. By deleting the redundant constraints on values for negative D_i we reach the phase diagram. shown in Figure 5.14. Of particular interest are the boundaries of region **B** ($D_2 = 3$ and $D_1 = 4$), both of which correspond to circular arcs in the space of the city; the boundaries of **AC** and **CD** are both hyperbolic ones.

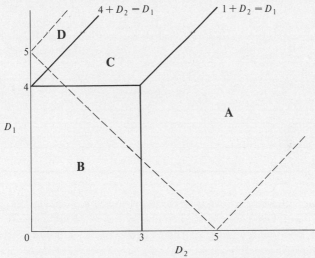

Fig. 5.14 Feasible solution regions with $\Gamma = 5$, with revised price data

We can also see how the set of solutions is affected as we alter the values of Γ (the distance between centres). At the limiting value of $\Gamma = 0$ the feasible set is merely the straight line through the origin at 45° to the axes. The set of solutions would include **A** and **B** only. As Γ is increased to 1 the set of solutions also includes **C**, and once Γ reaches 4 solution **D** is added. A further increase of Γ to 7 means that **B** drops out of the set of optimal solutions. However much more Γ is increased, solutions **A**, **C**, and **D** remain optimal for certain values. The feasibility boundaries with $\Gamma = 5$ are shown in Figure 5.14 as broken lines. These can then be transferred to the city map as in Figure 5.15. The solution boundary for **A** is outside the circle ($D_2 = 3$) and outside the hyperbola ($1 + D_2 = D_1$). The solution boundary for **B** is that area inside both circles ($D_1 = 4$, $D_2 = 3$). The solution boundary for **C** is outside the large circle ($D_1 = 4$)

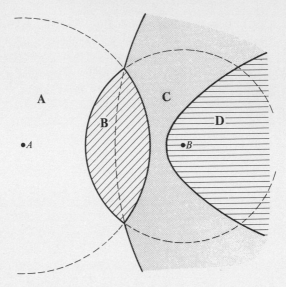

Fig. 5.15 Solution regions in a two-dimensional city for $\Gamma = 5$, with revised price data

and inside the hyperbola $(1 = D_2 = D_1)$ and outside the hyperbola $(4 + D_2 = D_1)$. For **D** it is the region inside the hyperbola $(4 + D_2 = D_1)$.

There are now several features of the two-dimensional phase diagram that are worth comment:

(i) The boundaries can be hyperbolic, straight lines, or circles. The last case has not been encountered before except in models where the transport cost schedules are different at different centres.

(ii) Because of the possibility of the existence of circular arcs the solution boundaries can intersect and this can produce solution regions that are very irregular in shape.

(iii) In the case of two centres and a homogeneous plane the solution map is the same above and below the axis joining the two centres.

(iv) It is not possible to calculate all the solution boundaries in the two-dimensional plane just from considering every boundary on the line joining the two centres. For example, the hyperbola $(1 + D_2 = D_1)$ does not bind as a boundary on the line joining centres A and B and therefore might be ignored. However, sufficiently far from the line, it divides regions **A** and **B**.

This analysis can be extended to the many-good case in a straight-forward fashion. The model is merely the two-parameter linear programme with an increased number of variables and requirement restrictions. The number of solution regions will increase just as in the one-dimensional case.

The final generalization to the two-dimensional many-centre case does raise one new problem. It seems that it would be possible to generate all solution boundaries either by a series of all pairwise calculations or by introducing three (or more) parameters. In this case the inequalities would be linear functions of the parameters D_1, D_2, and D_3. Obviously these three distances cannot be independent in two-dimensional space but in fact the actual mapping onto the city space imposes these restrictions automatically. A very simple example will serve to show how this works. Consider the one-good three-centre model with prices $p_A = 5$, $p_B = 6$, and $p_C = 4$ and a requirement of 1 unit. The general parametric programme is

$$X_0 - (D_1 + 5)X_1 - (D_2 + 6)X_2 - (D_3 + 4)X_3 = 0$$
$$X_1 \quad + \quad X_2 \quad + \quad X_3 = 1.$$

Entering X_3 into the basis by adding $(D_3 + 4)$ times row 2 to row 1 we have

$$X_0 - (D_1 + 1 - D_3)X_1 - (D_2 + 2 - D_3)X_2 + 0X_3 = D_3 + 4 \quad (5.41)$$

which is optimal for $X_3 = 1$ if

$$D_1 + 1 - D_3 > 0$$
$$D_2 + 2 - D_3 > 0.$$

We next let the second inequality fail and replace X_3 by X_2 to yield

$$X_0 - (D_1 - 1 - D_2)X_1 + 0X_2 + (D_2 + 2 - D_3)X_3 = D_2 + 6 \quad (5.42)$$

which is optimal for $X_2 = 1$ if

$$D_1 - 1 - D_2 > 0$$
$$D_3 - 2 - D_2 > 0.$$

Finally we enter X_1 and delete X_2 to obtain

$$X_0 - 0X_1 + (D_1 - 1 - D_2)X_2 + (D_1 - 1 - D_3)X_3 = D_1 + 5 \quad (5.43)$$

which is valid for $X_1 = 1$ if

$$D_2 + 1 - D_1 > 0$$
$$D_3 + 1 - D_1 > 0.$$

It can be seen that the three inequalities are consistent. If we consider the case when any two of them are equalities then the third is implied as an equality; this implies that if any pair of the hyperbolic arcs separating the centres meet then the third goes through the same point. Each hyperbolic arc or circle is orthogonal to the line joining the pair of centres implicit in the inequality.

A final point is that we can see that no inequality will involve all three distances (except in the degenerate case where a particular solution is valid only at a single point) because any line in the plane can be described by two coordinates.

CONCLUSION

We have seen how parametric linear programming can be used to determine solution regions in one- and two-dimensional cities for any number of goods and centres. From the structure of the fixed frequency model it emerges that all boundaries are hyperbolae or circles (straight lines when there are no price differentials).

The special structure of the linear programme used to model individual consumer choice means that certain solution variables will be optimal over a wide range of parameter values (rather than vary continuously). This in turn means that many consumers whose parameter values are sufficiently similar to each other will have identical optimal solutions to their shopping allocation problems. Since we have found a simple way of identifying ranges of parameter values that give identical solutions it follows that by treating distance as the single-variable parameter we are able to identify all those consumers in an area of a town that have the same shopping pattern. The trick, as in Chapter 3, is to recognize that the boundaries between solution regions define the behaviour of the consumers on either side, and hence the programme seeks to identify boundaries where different solutions nevertheless yield equal values of the objective function. This idea will be useful in Chapter 6 when we relax the assumption that frequencies are fixed and accordingly optimize over frequency and allocation at the same time.

One very suggestive feature of the model which we do not pursue is the invariance of the solutions in distance (D_i) space. This means that if we alter the location of a centre within the town the original solution phase diagram does not alter but that the mapping of these boundaries onto the town produces new market areas. However, it is clear that the boundaries shift in a fairly simple and easily predictable fashion as we consider simple variations—the location of the centre in question. This should make it possible to overcome the final problem identified by Eaton and Lipsey (1982) in their analysis— that is, to see how total demand shifts as the location of a shop varies. Once this is possible then the way would be open to find the equilibrium configuration of centres and shops.

6

THE ALLOCATION OF SHOPPING TRIPS AND DETERMINATION OF MARKET AREAS WHEN THE FREQUENCY OF SHOPPING IS A VARIABLE

The goal of this chapter is to integrate the themes developed separately in earlier chapters. We began our investigation into spatial consumer behaviour with a treatment of the complementary variable—the frequency of shopping. Chapters 2 and 3 analysed the determinants of the frequency of shopping for one and two goods for the case of a single shopping centre. By making several simplifications it was possible to demonstrate that often consumers would wish to purchase each good at a different frequency. This result justified the analysis in Chapter 4 of the allocation of shopping trips between centres in the many-good case when frequencies need not be identical. In order to use the very powerful results available to handle linear programmes the model investigated the case where frequency was fixed (and hence did not depend on which centre was actually used for the purchase of a good). In particular, it was possible to identify 'market areas' even for the most general cases and hence to provide a first step in moving towards equilibrium location analysis in the many-good case. However, it is clearly now necessary to integrate the two themes of choice over frequency and choice over location into a model which allows both to vary simultaneously. Such an approach is novel and it is likely that, since it combines the analytical difficulties of the two separate approaches, it will be increasingly difficult to obtain general results. In order to achieve any results at all it is necessary to use the simplest form of the models developed earlier in this book. The first section of this chapter focuses on the simultaneous choice of frequency and allocation of trips for a given consumer facing a choice between two centres in the one-good case. Market areas for the centres are then simple to derive. The second part of the chapter takes the critical step of generalizing the analysis to the simultaneous choice of frequency and allocation of trips for a given consumer in the two-centre two-good case.

This second section, which can be regarded as the very core of our study, has as its aim the demonstration that in the case of a hierarchy of centres, when frequency is a variable, some consumers will purchase from the lowest-order centre. This 'possibility' result is needed in order to establish that the consumer models developed could be consistent with the hierarchical structures of shopping centres that we have taken as a 'stylized fact'. The third part of the chapter analyses the determination of market areas in the two-good two-centre case. This step is crucial if even the simplest two-good equilibrium model is to be constructed using the models of this book.

FREQUENCY AND ALLOCATION FOR A CONSUMER FACING TWO CENTRES WITH A SINGLE GOOD

We begin with a single consumer facing a choice between two centres, both of which supply the single good required. The two centres are distinguished both by the 'mill' prices that they charge for the good and by the transport cost of travelling to them. Other costs, such as inventory costs or shopping costs, are assumed to be invariant between centres.

The specification of the consumer's objective turns out to be of critical importance later in this chapter. For the one-good case we analyse three of the models developed in Chapter 2 even though we shall use only one of these in the second and third sections of this chapter. The consumer's objectives are alternatively:

(i) cost minimization subject to a value requirement;
(ii) cost minimization subject to a quantity requirement;
(iii) utility maximization subject to an expenditure constraint.

For simplicity we concentrated on case (i) in Chapter 3, but since we can handle all three assumptions in the one-good case it is interesting to observe the variations between them. We investigate the three cases in turn using our basic three-cost model (purchase costs, inventory costs, and order costs).

(i) Cost minimization with a fixed value requirement

It is assumed that the consumer has a consumption requirement per day of V units (in value terms). The costs of shopping at the two centres (denoted A and B) are:

1. order costs, which consist of a pure shopping cost τ per trip to any centre plus a travel cost which is proportional to the distance to the centre (t_A or t_B);
2. inventory costs proportional to the average value held in the inventory per day;
3. purchase costs which depend on the prices charged at the two centres per physical unit (p_A or p_B).

From equation (2.3*) in Chapter 2 we have the results that if the consumer shops at centre A the cost-minimizing values are

$$f_A^* = \sqrt{\{cV/(t_A + \tau)\}}, \tag{6.1}$$

$$q_A^* = \sqrt{\{(t_A + \tau)V/cp_A^2\}}, \tag{6.2}$$

$$d_A^* = \sqrt{\{(t_A + \tau)/cV\}}, \tag{6.3}$$

with minimal total cost per period:

$$TC_A^* = V + 2\sqrt{cV(t_A + \tau)\}}. \tag{6.4}$$

Similarly, if the consumer were to shop at centre B the minimum total cost per period is

$$TC_B^* = V + 2\sqrt{\{cV(t_B + \tau)\}}. \tag{6.5}$$

As we have seen in Chapter 2, the minimum values for a given centre depend on all the parameters (t, τ, c, and V) except for the sale price (p). This price invariance property plays an important role in the analysis later so we consider it a little further now. It is produced by the fixed value requirements—it can be seen that such a requirement means that purchase costs are independent of prices (quantities per period are adjusted to offset prices). In order to offset the effect of higher prices on inventories the smaller bundles would be purchased to obtain constant values without any need to alter the number of trips per period. Hence the order cost element (which is independent of price) can be balanced against the inventory cost which can be made independent of price. Hence the only way to distinguish between the centres is the transport cost element and we can see that the consumer is indeed indifferent between centres when

$$t_A = t_B. \tag{6.6}$$

This locus for the market boundary in the variable frequency case should be compared with that obtained in the fixed frequency, 'no inventory cost' case:

$$p_A + t_A = p_B + t_B. \tag{6.7}$$

This latter model also assumes that a fixed quantity is purchased per trip (rather than a fixed value per period). In this latter case we can immediately establish the boundary by finding the point at which the cost of switching one trip to the other centre equals the cost of making that trip to the present centre. The variable frequency model does not permit such a simple, marginalistic calculation. As the equations (6.1) and (6.2) show, not only will we switch allocation of the boundary but also bundle size per trip will change (being inversely proportional to price). Hence the purchase cost of a trip is not proportional to price—the change in bundle size completely offsets it. Frequency is the same for both centres at the boundary. If transport costs are strictly proportional to distance then the boundary is half-way between the two centres.

(ii) Cost minimization with a fixed quantity requirement

The model considered is exactly the same as for case (i) except that the consumer requires a fixed quantity (Q) of consumption per period (instead of a fixed value). The results of Chapter 2 yield the optimum values for shopping at centre A:

$$f_A^* = \sqrt{\{cQp_A/(t_A + \tau)\}}, \tag{6.8}$$

$$d_A^* = \sqrt{\{(t_A + \tau)/cQp_A\}}, \tag{6.9}$$

$$q_A^* = \sqrt{\{(t_A + \tau)Q/cp_A\}}, \tag{6.10}$$

with minimum cost of

$$TC_A^* = p_A Q + 2\sqrt{\{cp_A Q(t_A + \tau)\}}. \tag{6.11}$$

Similarly, the minimum cost of shopping at B is:

$$TC_B^* = p_B Q + 2\sqrt{\{cp_B Q(t_B + \tau)\}}. \tag{6.12}$$

The consumer is indifferent between the centres when equation (6.11) is equal to equation (6.12), and this defines an equation of the locus (in bi-polar coordinates t_A and t_B) of the market boundary. If prices are equal then, as before, this is a straight line half-way between the centres. However, when prices are not equal there is a new shape to the boundary. This does not appear to be that of any well-established curve and would need to be investigated in some detail to establish the possible forms for the market boundary. It is clear, however, that prices can have a strong effect on the location of the boundary if they are sufficiently different.

(iii) Utility maximization with an expenditure constraint

The same cost function as before is used, but now the consumer aims to maximize utility (that is, quantity bought per period) subject to an income constraint. The results of Chapter 2 indicate that the utility-maximizing solutions for shopping at centre A are

$$f_A^* = -c + \sqrt{\{c^2 + cY/(t_A + t)\}}, \tag{6.13}$$

$$q_A^* = -(t_A + \tau) + \sqrt{\{(t_A + \tau)^2 + (t_A + \tau)Y/c\}}, \tag{6.14}$$

$$Q_A^* = [Y - 2\sqrt{\{c^2(t_A + \tau)^2 + c(t_A + \tau)Y\}}]/p_A. \tag{6.15}$$

Similar equations hold for the utility-maximizing pattern of shopping at centre B. The consumer is indifferent where the utility levels are equal (i.e. where $Q_A^* = Q_B^*$). The locus of the market boundary is again a complicated function but is obviously price sensitive. When prices are equal the boundary is again midway between the two centres.

The analysis of these three cases highlights immediately the great gain in simplicity from using the fixed value assumption. It is also true, however, that the second and third cases, although giving different solutions for frequencies and quantities, do yield progressively similar market boundaries as the price differential narrows. This is perhaps an important consideration for future research—to see to what extent the locational aspects of the model are affected by the choice of consumer objectives. For the rest of this chapter we will stick to the fixed value requirement case. The prime justification for this is that it simplifies without appearing to lose any of the essentials of our models.

In discussing these three cases no attention has been paid to the integrality constraints on frequency that were so important in

Chapter 5. Of course, the single-good nature of the problem does not force the issue as in the case of two or more goods, but it is nevertheless possible to consider how case (i) could be restricted to integer frequencies and durations. The approach would be to establish conditions for the various integer frequencies to be optimal. Since the cost function is concave in f (or d):

$$TC = V + \frac{cV}{f} + tf \qquad (6.16)$$

then an integer frequency is the optimal integer frequency if and only if it has a lower cost than the two neighbouring integer frequencies, i.e. if

$$TC(n-1) > TC(n) < TC(n+1). \qquad (6.17)$$

This implies that for

$$n(n-1)(t+\tau) < cV < n(n+1)(t+\tau) \qquad (6.18)$$

the integer frequency n is optimal. These inequalities allow us, for τ, c, and V, to derive the optimal integer frequencies (and durations). Once this is done the associated bundle sizes can be derived from the value requirement, and costs from equation (6.16). It should be noted that the boundary between two centres will be unaffected by the restriction to integer frequencies. Since the cost functions are entirely symmetric, the costs of the integer-constrained cost functions will be equal for a distance half-way between the two centres.

Finally, we note that the extension of this discussion to the many-centre case would mirror that of the fixed frequency analysis in Chapter 2. With a one-dimensional (linear) town all market boundaries would be half-way between adjacent shopping centres, while in a two-dimensional town the boundaries are given by the intersection of straight lines orthogonal to lines joining each pair of centres and equidistant from the pair of centres in question.

FREQUENCY AND ALLOCATION FOR A CONSUMER FACING TWO CENTRES IN THE TWO-GOOD CASE

Although at the end of our analysis of this case it will become apparent that great simplifications are possible, it will be much easier to follow a step-by-step argument. This means that we discuss, one by one, all the possible patterns of shops and shopping trips and then decide how to choose, for a given pattern of shops, between the different shopping programmes that could be carried out.

We firstly subdivide the model into the three distinct patterns of availability:

(i) each centre sells a single and different good;
(ii) both centres sell both goods;
(iii) one centre (call it *A*) sells both goods and the other (*B*) sells just one good.

These three patterns encompass a model with no agglomeration where each good is sold at a specialized centre (case (i)), a model with complete agglomeration where all goods are sold at every centre (case (ii)), and the interesting intermediate hierarchical structure (case (iii)) where some centres are of higher order and sell a wider range of goods. Our aim is to show how case (iii) might come about, so that it will be of critical importance to determine consumer behaviour and market boundaries for the hierarchy.

(i) Each good sold by a separate centre

When all centres are completely specialized and there can be no competition between rival sellers of the same good then analysis is trivial. We can optimize separately for each good according to the principles of the first section. With no multi-purpose trips possible the costs are completely independent and so is the use of the two different centres. Obviously each centre collects all the trade for its good from the whole town. The generalization to many goods and many centres, where the only restriction is that no centre sells more than one good, is the same as for the one-good case, just repeated for each of the goods in turn.

(ii) Both goods supplied by both centres

The case where both centres supply both goods (i.e. there has been agglomeration without hierarchy emerging) permits the largest number of patterns of shopping. There are four distinct arrangements:

(*a*) both goods bought solely at one centre;
(*b*) both goods bought at one centre and one good also purchased at the other centre;

(*c*) each good bought at a different centre;
(*d*) both goods bought at both centres.

Within these types of shopping programme there are further permutations as the linking of goods to centres is changed. Case (*a*) has two permutations (both at centre *A* or both at *B*); case (*b*) has four; case (*c*) has two, and case (*d*) has just one. These nine separate cases will clearly all have different cost functions, so that at first sight the type of analysis used in Chapter 3 would have to be repeated nine times to identify the minimum cost frequency for each allocation and then the nine conditional minima be compared to identify the global minimum. However, the particular structure of the cost functions means that the problem can be simplified in two cases, each of which is straightforward to handle. The key argument is that pertaining to the irrelevance of prices in this model with respect to costs. As we have seen, the cost-minimizing model with a value constraint produces a total cost function that is independent of prices. Hence the sole factors that will decide between centres are the distance costs and the availability of the goods. In the case where all goods are supplied at every centre availability is not a discriminating factor—no consumer chooses one centre or the other because of the range of goods. This immediately allows us to see that if one good is preferred to be purchased from centre *A* then both goods will be, since the same factors operate in both cases. *A fortiori*, the possibility of sharing travel costs on multi-purpose trips will as usual tend to tie frequencies together. This simple argument rules out arrangements (*b*), (*c*), and (*d*) and so there are no multi-centre shopping programmes when all centres supply the same range of goods. Further, anticipating our discussion of market areas, we can see that since distance is the discriminating factor the consumer will buy all goods, whether on single-purpose or multi-purpose trips, at the nearest centre. This prediction which, as we have pointed out in Chapter 1, is very unsatisfactory, can be seen to re-emerge in our model when there is no hierarchy of centres. It is not just a feature of the earlier single-purpose trip assumption.

The choice for a given consumer between the centres is then between the minimum cost programme of shopping at centre *A* and that of shopping at centre *B*. The cost functions, as shown in Chapter 5, do depend on whether the frequencies of buying the goods stand in an integer multiple relationship. Thus for shopping at *A* the total costs are given by

$$FI(A) = [(t_A + 2\tau) + \{(d_2/d_1) - 1\}(t_A + \tau)]/d_2$$
$$+ cV_1d_1 + cV_2d_2 + V_1 + V_2 \qquad (6.19)$$

for d_2 an integer multiple of d_1, and

$$FN(A) = [(t_A + 2\tau)h + (d_1 + d_2 - 2h)(t_A + \tau)]/d_1d_2$$
$$+ cV_1d_1 + cV_2d_2 + V_1 + V_2 \qquad (6.20)$$

for d_2 not an integer multiple of d_1, for d_1 and d_2 integer, and where h is the HCF of d_1 and d_2. The functions for shopping at centre B are identical except that t_B replaces t_A throughout.

The complete symmetry between the two sets of cost functions means that the boundary of preference between the centres is at $t_A = t_B$. Subject to this restriction we can first decide where the consumer shops and then apply the inequalities developed in Chapter 3 (Table 3.1) to obtain the optimal frequencies for any given consumer.

(iii) Both goods supplied by one centre and one good by the other

This is in many ways the most interesting case for our purposes since it is the simplest hierarchical structure and so the principles involved in its analysis will give valuable insights into whether such structures can survive when faced by consumer demand of a non-single-purpose shopping trip nature.

For such a configuration of centres and shops there are three distinct types of shopping programme:

(*a*) both goods bought solely at the higher-order centre (a single-centre programme);

(*b*) both goods bought at the higher-order centre and also the single good bought at the lower-order centre (a multi-centre programme);

(*c*) the good unique to the higher-order centre bought there and the common good bought at the lower-order centre (a multi-centre programme).

However, one of these cases can immediately be ruled out. Since prices play no part in the decision-making of a consumer shopping subject to constant value requirements, then only transport costs decide allocation. Since the consumer must always make trips to centre A to buy the good (call it 2) which is found only there then the effective transport cost of buying good 1 there on the same occasion (and reducing by the same amount the number of trips made to centre B for good 1) will be zero. This must always be a transport cost saving unless the consumer is located actually at B, and hence no programme which does not use these multi-purpose trips can be optimal. Thus the choice is simply between cases (a) and (b).

We handle this as for the case where both centres sell both goods. The two sets of cost functions are separately minimized and we then choose that case which gives the lower of the two conditional minima.

(a) Both goods purchased at centre A

The cost functions and boundaries are again exactly as for the model developed in Chapter 3 and also used for the case where both centres sell both goods:

$$FI(A) = [(t_A + 2\tau) + \{(d_2/d_1 - 1)\}(t_A + \tau)]/d_2$$
$$+ cV_1 d_1 + cV_2 d_2 + V_1 + V_2 \qquad (6.21)$$

where d_2 is an integer multiple of d_1, and

$$FN(A) = [(t_A + 2\tau)h + (d_1 + d_2 - 2h)(t_A + \tau)]/d_1 d_2$$
$$+ cV_1 d_1 + cV_2 d_2 + V_1 + V_2 \qquad (6.22)$$

where d_2 is not an integer multiple of d_1, h is the HCF of d_1 and d_2, and d_1 and d_2 are integer. (As usual this formulation is for the case $V_1 > V_2$.) The conditional solution boundaries are exactly as generated by Table 13.1 of Chapter 3, so that for the particular parameter values $cV_1 = 4$, $cV_2 = 1$ we obtain Table 6.1.

(b) Both goods purchased at centre A and good 1 also purchased at centre B

Although there may at first sight appear to be a large number of patterns of shopping programme when there is a hierarchy of centres, in fact several cases can be ruled out by appeal to general arguments. First, it is important to note that the good supplied at the lower-order centre can only be good 1 (that with the higher value requirement). This is because the total number of trips for good 1 must be greater or equal to the total number of trips for good 2. Since all possible trips to centre A can be multi-purpose (the effective

TABLE 6.1

Critical inequalities in a hierarchical model if both
goods are purchased at the higher-order centre
$(cV_1 = 4, cV_2 = 1)$

Combination		Inequalities
d_1	d_2	
1	1	$\tau < 2$
		$t_A + 2\tau < 10$
1	2	$\tau > 2$
		$\tau < 6$
		$t_A + \tau < 8$
1	3	$\tau > 6$
		$\tau < 12$
		$t_A + \tau < 12$
		$3t_A + 2\tau < 18$
		$6t_A + 7\tau < 60$
		$2t_A + 3\tau < 24$
2	2	$t_A + \tau > 8$
		$\tau < 8$
		$3t_A + 2\tau > 8$
		$t_A + 2\tau < 30$
		$\tau - t_A < 6$
		$t_A + 2\tau > 10$
2	3	$2t_A + 3\tau > 24$
		$2t_A + \tau < 24$
		$\tau - t_A > 6$
		$2t_A + \tau < 12$

transport cost for the good supplied at both centres being zero on
the occasions on which the unique good is purchased at centre A),
only the excess of the higher frequency over the lower need be purchased at centre B. This rules out good 2 from ever being supplied
at the lower-order centre (the need to shop for good 1 at the higher-
order centre will generate enough free transport trips for all of the
requirements of good 2 to be purchased at the higher-order centre).
This argument limits us to one pattern of hierarchical supply in the
two-good case. Another possibility that is ruled out is a programme
in which there are some single-purpose trips for good 1 to centre A
and some other single-purpose trips for good 1 to centre B—these
are equivalent operations differing only in transport costs and hence
one or other always dominates. This leaves two cases, depending on

whether the two frequencies are in an integer multiple relation or not.

If the frequencies of purchase are in an integer multiple relationship then the pattern of shopping is of a form illustrated in Table 6.2. The total cost per period in such a case is

$$FI = [(t_A + 2\tau) + (t_B + \tau)\{(d_2/d_1) - 1\}]/d_2$$
$$+ cV_1d_1 + cV_2d_2 + V_1 + V_2 \qquad (6.23)$$

for d_2 an integer multiple of d_1.

When the frequencies are not in an integer multiple relationship the pattern is of a type illustrated by Table 6.3. Good 1 is purchased every other day which good 2 is purchased every three days. There is an opportunity for a multi-purpose trip to centre A every six days. The total cost per day is given by

$$FN = [(t_A + 2\tau)h + (d_1 - h)(t_A + \tau)$$
$$+ (d_2 - h)(t_B + \tau)]/d_1d_2 + cV_1d_1 + cV_2d_2$$
$$+ V_1 + V_2 \qquad (6.24)$$

where d_2 is not an integer multiple of d_1, where h is the HCF of d_1 and d_2, and d_1 and d_2 are integer.

The pair of functions (6.23), (6.24) is similar to those for the single-centre, two-good model developed in Chapter 3. In particular

TABLE 6.2

A shopping pattern for integer multiple frequencies using both centres in the hierarchical case

Day	1	2	3	4	5	6
Good 1 purchased at centre	A	B	A	B	A	B
Good 2 purchased at centre	A	—	A	—	A	—

TABLE 6.3

A shopping pattern for non-integer multiple frequencies using both centres in the hierarchical case

Day	1	2	3	4	5	6
Good 1 purchased at centre	A	—	B	—	B	—
Good 2 purchased at centre	A	—	—	A	—	—

the functions satisfy the three conditions:

  (i) $FI\,(x\,y) < FN\,(x\,y)$ (for each x and y);
 (ii) FI is additive;
(iii) FI is concave.

Given these three properties, exactly the same algorithm as in the single-centre case can be used to generate inequalities which must hold for a particular solution to be optimal. This means that the list of function comparisons is exactly the same as in Table 3.1 of Chapter 3. However, since the actual functions used are different, the actual inequalities for the comparison of two solutions will take a different value. Using the same parameter values as in Chapter 3 ($cV_1 = 4$, $cV_2 = 1$) we can derive the critical inequalities for a hierarchy of centres conditional on both centres being used. Table 6.4 presents some values.

A very important aspect of the latter cost functions is that they have been calculated for the case where $d_1 = d_2$ on which just multi-purpose trips to centre A are used. Inspection shows that the value of function (6.24) collapses back to that of function (6.23) in such a case, i.e. that the cost has been correctly ascertained. Hence the inequalities in Table 6.4 genuinely compare multi-centre trips ($d_1 \neq d_2$) to single-centre trips ($d_1 = d_2$). This aspect will make the comparison of the two conditional minima a little less straightforward. Comparing the two sets of cost curves we can see that (6.21) $\leq$ (6.23) and (6.22) $\leq$ (6.24) for any given combination if and only if $t_A < t_B$. This suggests at first sight that we have the same type of result as before, i.e. that the consumer does all his shopping at A if he is nearer to it than B, and if not he uses both centres. However, this is not quite correct. Since for cases $d_1 = d_2$ the allocation under both sets of cost curves is in fact for all shopping to be done at centre A, it does not follow that if $t_A > t_B$ the costs will indicate that both centres will be used. If the cost functions (6.23) and (6.24) indicate that an equal frequency case is optimal then all shopping at centre A is still better than shopping at both centres. Hence the procedure is first to allocate all trips to A if $t_A \leq t_B$ and find the optimal frequencies using functions (6.21) and (6.22) and the associated inequalities. If $t_A > t_B$ we first check whether an equal frequency case is optimal from Table 6.4-type inequalities. If so, all shopping is allocated to centre A at these frequencies and if not, a multi-centre programme is optimal, with frequencies indicated by Table 6.4.

TABLE 6.4

Critical inequalities for a hierarchy of centres when both centres are used ($cV_1 = 4$, $cV_2 = 1$)

Combination		Inequalities
d_1	d_2	
1	1	$t_A + \tau - t_B < 2$
		$t_A + 2\tau < 10$
1	2	$t_A + \tau - t_B > 2$
		$t_A + \tau - t_B < 6$
		$\tau + t_B < 8$
1	3	$t_A + \tau - t_B > 6$
		$t_A + \tau - t_B < 12$
		$\tau + t_B < 24$
		$t_A + 2\tau + 2t_B < 60$
		$3\tau + 2t_B < 24$
2	2	$\tau + t_B > 8$
		$t_A + \tau - t_B < 8$
		$t_A + 2\tau > 10$
		$t_A + 2\tau + 2t_B > 18$
		$t_A + 2\tau < 30$
		$t_A + \tau - 2t_B < 6$
2	3	$3\tau + 2t_B > 24$
		$\tau + 2t_B < 24$
		$t_A + \tau - 2t_B > 6$
		$t_A + \tau + t_B < 12$

The inequalities of Table 6.4 reveal the fact that for consumers living nearer to the lower-order centre there can be conditions under which they will use it as well as the higher-order centre. This demonstrates that multi-centre shopping programmes are possible in the hierarchical case, so that we can answer the first part of the question as to the economic viability of lower-order centres—they do capture some trade. Whether they can capture enough trade depends of course on the size of their market area, and we return to this question later. An important feature of the hierarchical case (as with the fixed frequency model of Chapter 4) is that not all shopping for a good is necessarily done at the nearest centre selling it. Our model, then, is consistent with two key empirical observations:

(*a*) some shopping trips are multi-purpose;
(*b*) not all shopping has to be done at the nearest source of supply.

The arguments given in the last two subsections have shown how to determine allocation and frequency for an individual consumer. An important result has emerged. If the consumer lives nearer to a centre selling all goods than to any other centre, then no other centre will be used in the shopping programme. This result, which makes frequency and allocation almost sequential decisions, is entirely due to the fixed value requirements. If there were instead fixed quantity requirements, then price differentials between centres would modify the allocation decision considerably. It is apparent, however, that for a fixed quantity requirement without price differentials the results would coincide with those for fixed values. For the utility-maximizing model price differentials intra- and inter-centres will be important in determining location and so, even without price differentials for a given good, the solutions will not be of the simple form derived in this chapter.

We next turn to the construction of market areas for the various patterns of centres for the two-good case.

MARKET AREAS IN THE TWO-CENTRE TWO-GOOD CASE WHEN FREQUENCY IS A VARIABLE

The joint optimization of allocation and frequency did seem at first sight to be a formidable task, so that the determination of market areas might have been expected to be a problem of some complexity. However, we have seen that, when the consumer optimizes subject to a fixed value requirement, there are fairly simply solutions for the individual. The key result is that allocation and frequency are independent of prices charged, so that only availability and transport costs matter. Hence it is likely that market area determination will follow in a straightforward fashion. The three patterns of shopping centre for the two-good two-centre case are taken in turn.

(i) Each good supplied by a different centre

In this trivial case every consumer in the town (whether it is one- or two-dimensional) buys all his requirements from the sole centre selling the good. The market area for each shop is the whole town and the value of sales is the value per consumer times the area of the town times the consumer density.

(ii) Both goods supplied by both centres

The analysis for the individual consumer has shown that all shopping will be done at the nearest centre. Hence the market area boundary is a line equidistant from the two centres (i.e. a straight line half-way between the two centres and orthogonal to a line joining them). Each shop at each centre captures an amount of trade proportional to the area of the town cut off by the orthogonal bisector to the centres and, with a regular-shaped city with centres symmetrically placed, each shop of a given type will capture the same amount of trade.

(iii) Hierarchical structure of supply

The higher-order centre supplying both goods we call A and the lower-order centre supplying just good 1 we call B. The discussion of the individual consumer's behaviour in this case makes it clear that not only does centre A capture all the trade in the town for good 2, but that it captures all the trade in good 1 from those consumers living nearer to it than to centre B and also *some* trade from all consumers living nearer to centre B (when they make multipurpose trips to centre A for the purchase of good 2). In addition there can be circumstances where some of the consumers living nearer to B nevertheless do all of their shopping for good 1 at centre A (i.e. they make nothing but multi-purpose trips to centre A). The exact pattern does depend on the actual values of the parameters, and we can illustrate for certain sets of values.

We begin with the values $\tau = 1$, $cV_1 = 4$, and $cV_2 = 1$. The critical inequalities derived from Table 6.4 are plotted in Figure 6.1. For the parameter values chosen, the solution (2 3) is never optimal whatever the position of the centres with respect to each other or to the market. Further, for any combinations for which $t_A \leq t_B$ the multi-centre programmes used to derive the solution regions will never be optimal. A dashed line shows the region in which multi-centre shopping might be optimal for those consumers who do not live closer to A than to B. It can indeed be seen that for some combinations above the dotted line the consumers, despite living nearer to B than to A, will nevertheless do all their shopping at A on multi-purpose trips (for example solution regions (1 1) and (2 2) above the dashed line). Other consumers will use both centres. For example, a consumer in solution region (1 2) will use centre A once every two days for a multi-purpose trip and on the other days will buy good 1 at centre B. Half of the trade for good 1 in this region then goes to centre A. Further away from the equal-distance line (i.e. relatively

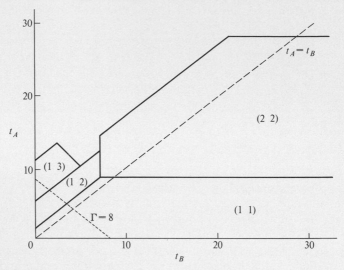

Fig. 6.1 Solution regions for two goods and a two-centre hierarchy with variable frequencies ($\tau = 1$, $cV_1 = 4$, $cV_2 = 1$)

nearer to centre B), in the (1 3) region, it will become optimal to shop once every three days at centre A for both goods and on the other two days to buy good 1 at centre B—only one-third of the trade in good 1 will go to centre A in this zone.

The map of solution regions expressed in bi-polar coordinates is invariant with respect to the actual locations of the centres concerned (as in Chapter 5). However, just as before, it is possible to derive the solution and market boundaries only when the location of the centres within the town is specified. For two centres Γ units apart the set of solutions can be derived. We consider first a linear town.

(a) Market demands in a linear town with a hierarchical structure

For the area *between* the two centres when they are Γ units apart the set of possible combinations is given by the line

$$t_A + t_B = \Gamma. \tag{6.25}$$

For a given value of Γ, Figure 6.1 yields all the solution regions. Suppose that $\Gamma = 8$, then up to $t_A = 4$ all trade goes to centre A irrespective of the other parameter values. Also in this case, for a value of t_A up to 4.5 (where $t_A + t_B = 8$ intersects $t_A - t_B = 1$) all shopping continues to go to centre A. From $t_A = 4.5$ up to $t_A = 6.5$, one trip every two days is made to A for both goods and one trip every other day to centre B for good 1. From $t_A = 6.5$ up to $t_A = 8$ there is one trip every three days to centre A for both goods, and trips on each of the other two days to centre B for good 1.

The areas of the town not between the centres are generated by the equation

$$|t_A - t_B| = \Gamma \tag{6.26}$$

subject to maxima and minima on t_A and t_B. If the town extends for 1 unit either side of the centres then the maximum values are t_A, $t_B = 9$. It can be seen that for the consumers in the area to the right of centre B the shopping programme will continue to lie in solution region (1 3), with two-thirds of the trade in good 1 going to centre B. The complete market demand function for good 1 is shown in Figure 6.2, which illustrates the complex relationship between trade and distance in the hierarchical case. There can be a series of sharp boundaries at which trade to centre A for good 1 falls by discrete amounts. In particular, centre A attracts all the trade in good 1 from an area which is nearer to centre B than to itself.

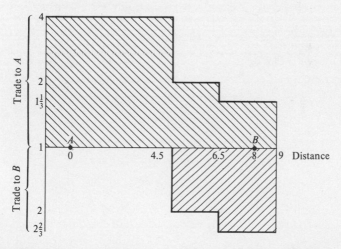

Fig. 6.2 Demand cones for good 1 in the two-good case with a two-centre hierarchy for $\Gamma = 8$

There is also one further unexpected result which can be seen as we vary Γ. This is of course an interesting parametric variation, since it corresponds to the location decision of the single shop once centre A has been established. For the case we have considered ($\tau = 1$, $cV_1 = 4$, $cV_2 = 1$), Figure 6.1 shows that for $\Gamma \leq 1$ centre B can gain no trade. At $\Gamma = 2$ we see that the solution regions between the centres switch from doing all the good 1 shopping at A, to doing half the good 1 shopping at B and half at A. Beyond B (as we move along the line $t_A + t_B = 2$) the pattern of solution remains the same until we reach the point $t_A = 9$, $t_B = 7$, where the optimal solution switches to (2 2), i.e. all shopping for both goods is done on trips every other day to centre A. The market demand for this case is shown in Figure 6.3 (assuming that the length of the town is 10 and that A locates at the left-hand edge). The reason why the trade beyond B eventually all reverts to centre A is that the increasing effects of distance become so strong that joint trips will offset any inventory gains that might occur from shopping at different frequencies.

It can also be seen that as Γ increases the trade captured by centre B behaves in a complicated fashion. As we have remarked, at the point $\Gamma = 1$, centre B just captures one-half of the trade to the right up to a distance 8 units away (14 units in all). At $\Gamma = 2$ we have seen that centre B captures half the trade between coordinates 1.5 and 9 (15 units). At $\Gamma = 3$ it captures a maximum of 16 units (between

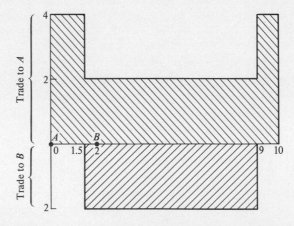

Fig. 6.3 Demand cones for good 1 in the two-good case with a two-centre hierarchy for $\Gamma = 2$

coordinates 2 and 10). If it were to move further away, for example $\Gamma = 4$, it can make no further gains on the right of the town and loses trade to A on the left. Hence the optimum location, given centre A, is at a point 3 units to the left of centre A. This case has two interesting aspects. First, it may not be profitable to attempt to approach too close to centre A. This is in sharp distinction to the one-good model, where the optimal strategy would be to approach as closely as possible. This is a result of some generality. The reason why it happens is that centre A attracts all the trade from further away than the half-way point between the two centres, and the closer the two centres the further this region extends. From equation (6.23) we see that there will be a solution boundary between (1 1) and (1 2) at

$$t_A = t_B - \tau + 2cV_1. \qquad (6.27)$$

Hence for $t_A > t_B$ we require

$$2cV_1 > \tau. \qquad (6.28)$$

Under this condition the boundary between the centres is more than half-way between the centres, and by approaching too close centre B would lose all its trade.

The example also shows that there is a second reason why centre B may not wish to approach too close to centre A. It is losing the chance of capturing more trade at extreme distances beyond B than it can gain as it approaches A. There can be a definite optimum location which will depend on the relative values of the parameters of the model.

(b) *Market demands in a two-dimensional town*

The establishment of the market boundaries in a two-dimensional town uses analogous methods to the one-dimensional case and again draws on the techniques of Chapter 5. The solution boundaries are no longer points, but curves. For the case we have been considering (Figure 6.1) there is a boundary between (1 1) and (1 2) on a line $t_A - t_B = 1$ for values of t_A between 1 and 8, and a boundary between (1 2) and (2 2) on a line $t_b = 7$ (for $8 \le t_A \le 12$) etc. The first boundary is a hyperbolic one and the second a circular one. If we take a town which has (for the given location of centre A) a maximum value of $t_A = 9$, then there are only three solution regions indicated for $t_A > t_B$ and $\Gamma < 5$. We illustrate the solution regions for the case of $\Gamma = 2$ in Figure 6.4, which shows that centre B captures one-half of the trade in good 1 from all the shaded area and centre A captures the other half. Centre A also captures all the trade in good 1 from the rest of the town. It can also be seen that the frequency of shopping at A is less for consumers well beyond B than it is for those between A and B but living nearer to B. The rest of the frequencies to the left of the equidistance line can be determined by reference to Table 6.1.

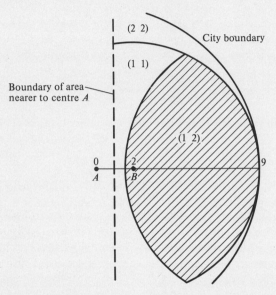

Fig. 6.4 Solution regions in the two-good case with a two-centre hierarchy in a two-dimensional city for $\Gamma = 2$

Variations in market area as centre B shifts its location relative to centre A can be determined as before, although the analysis will be more complicated. It will still be the case that it may lose trade if it approaches too close to centre A.

The extension to three centres should be straightforward. The use of pairwise comparisons, although perhaps laborious, is quite simple using the ideas developed here.

CONCLUSION

In this chapter we have been able to show how to derive the simultaneous choice over frequency and location for a consumer in the two-good two-centre case. The analysis was greatly simplified by the effect of the constant value requirement assumption. This assumption allowed us to analyse the choice between centres and over frequency in a sequential fashion. For all cases, except that of consumers living nearer to the lower-order centre when there is a hierarchy, shoppers will certainly do all their shopping at the nearest centre providing the good. The frequencies can be determined as if there were just a single centre to consider. For those shoppers living nearer to the lower-order centre it may still be cheaper to do all their shopping at the higher-order centre on multi-purpose trips. The extent to which this is true will determine the amount of trade attracted by the lower-order centre and hence whether it can survive.

A very important aspect of these results is that if the lower-order centre locates too close to the higher-order centre it will do no trade at all. This prevents a difficulty that is present when two centres of the same order are concerned. In the latter case, as the second centre approaches the first it captures more and more trade and hence some location models have produced unsatisfactory results by predicting location as close as possible to the existing centre. In the hierarchical case there is clearly an optimal location for the lower-order centre. If it is too far from the higher-order centre and is therefore near the edge of the town it has foregone trade towards the centre that it could have captured. If, on the other hand, it approaches the higher-order centre too closely it will gain no further trade from consumers located between the two centres and may lose trade from the periphery of the city—once travel costs are high the consumer is pushed more towards making multi-purpose trips whenever possible and hence uses just the higher-order centre.

Hence, although our model of the consumer is based upon a simple view of his behaviour, and clearly ignores some important aspects of choice over frequency, we have been able to construct a theory of choice over space that produces predictions of behaviour that are a distinct improvement on the single-purpose/nearest centre assumption of 'central place' theory. When hierarchical structures of shops exist then some consumers do not purchase a good at the nearest source of supply and some will, indeed, use more than one centre to purchase certain goods. At the same time multi-purpose trips are often used and will be important in directing some trade away from the nearest source of supply. Even for consumers with identical location patterns, there may be variations in the frequency of the purchase of the goods.

Now that we have constructed an integrated spatial choice model we can see the crucial role played by the frequency of shopping. Only when frequencies are different can lower-order centres survive once there are any possible economies from buying more than one good at the same time from a given centre. In turn, we have seen that frequency will be the same when there is no shopping cost element to using a centre but only a transport cost which is independent of the number of goods purchased at a centre. Accordingly, the higher the relative costs of transport (as opposed to costs of shopping) the more likely frequencies are to be equalized and the less trade will be done by lower-order centres. As transport costs weaken the frequencies of purchase of the different goods separate and the possible success of lower-order centres increases. The existence of hierarchies is then largely dependent in our model on the relative importance of the two aspects of order costs. The construction of purpose-built shopping centres which not only are attractive by being of high order but also are often designed to make the actual shopping as easy as possible, thereby lowering the shopping cost element, will draw trade away from lower-order centres even though consumers live nearer to such centres. This line of analysis could be followed in detail for the simple cases considered in detail in this chapter.

Although we have arrived at our main aim, that of constructing a model of consumer choice of the allocation of shopping, not only has this model simplified the choice structure greatly (which may not matter too much for the purpose of gaining insights into spatial behaviour) but is has also neglected certain dimensions of spatial behaviour. In particular, the question of modal choice concerns all those working on spatial behaviour and it is of interest to see how the basic models can be extended to provide some analysis of the choice between transport modes when several are available.

Chapter 7 not only constructs some simple modal choice models but also indicates under what circumstances modal choice and location choice will interact, thus pointing to an even more general model of consumer choice than that considered so far.

7

SHOPPING PATTERNS AND THE CHOICE OF TRANSPORT MODE

Although the central theme of this book is the effect of distance on consumer behaviour, we have so far taken a very simple view of the way in which distance is involved in consumer choice. Specifically, we have concentrated on the costs of travelling the distance from the point of origin to the shop. In doing so we have explicitly assumed that transport costs to any centre are strictly proportional to the distance between the consumer's residence and the centre, and that all consumers start shopping trips from the home. Both assumptions, although convenient for analysis, restrict our understanding of individual behaviour and of the determinants of market areas.

We need to be able to consider a much wider range of possibilities. Three types of case stand out as being of interest. For some consumers, the effective transport costs per mile to different centres are not equal. The classic example of this phenomenon is where one centre is linked by a bus route passing the consumer's home while the other is not. If the consumer has to walk in one direction but can catch a bus in the other, then it may be that the consumer would be prepared to travel much farther by bus than on foot to buy a given bundle of goods. We need to be able to discuss more carefully the relation between the mode chosen and the per unit distance transport cost, and then to analyse the effects of asymmetric transport provision.

A second case, which is perhaps even more interesting in the analysis of modal choice, is that where the consumer has available several alternative modes of travel for a given centre. In this context, the restricted availability of certain modes is a rich source of analysis. As well as modal choice at a given distance we are also concerned to discuss whether modal choice will vary with distance and, accordingly, whether shifts in transport cost parameters will affect modal choice and even allocation decisions.

The third aspect is the relation between shopping and other activities. Much shopping is done in trips from the place of work, which may then give a very different relation between distance travelled and location then the home/shop relation. Also, shopping is often combined with a trip to a centre for a non-shopping activity (a 'joint-purpose' trip), such as a visit to a library. These generalizations are worthy of some study since they do influence shopping behaviour and hence will affect location decisions. At the same time we do not have the space to apply all these generalizations to all the cases we have so far studied, and only a handful of cases can be looked at in detail.

MODAL CHOICE TO A SINGLE CENTRE WHEN MORE THAN ONE MODE IS AVAILABLE

We begin by studying the case of a single consumer buying just one good from a given centre when there is more than one transport mode available. Clearly, per unit distance costs will be a major factor in discriminating between modes but the factors influencing the choice will be affected by the structure of the model.

The simplest case we analyse is that where the consumer minimizes the sum of the three costs (purchase, order, and storage) subject to a value requirement. In this case, mode can affect only the order cost element through its relationship with distance. In the utility-maximizing framework, modal choice could depend on what factors we assumed to affect the level of utility. If the amount of leisure or disutility of carrying heavy bundles is allowed for then the mode will be chosen that also best takes these factors into consideration.

In the cost-minimizing model the consumer is required to minimize the per unit time period cost of purchasing subject to a value requirement. If there are two modes of transport available to the given centre then at any given distance one or the other will have a lower cost per trip and that mode will be chosen, i.e. the consumer must minimize

$$TC_1 = pqf + t_1 f + cpq$$

or

$$TC_2 = pqf + t_2 f + cpq \tag{7.1}$$

with

$$V = pqf$$

where t_i is the total cost (transport and shopping) associated with a trip by mode i. Clearly, the lower t_i is chosen and this gives the standard results

$$f^* = \sqrt{(cV/t_i)} \tag{7.2}$$

$$q^* = \sqrt{(t_i V/cp^2)}. \tag{7.3}$$

The extension of this analysis to all consumers depends critically on the relation between distance and transport costs. Studies of individual shopping behaviour, for example Bacon (1968), have shown a significant switch in modal choice for consumers visiting a centre with increasing distance, so that the choice appears to be distance-related.

In models which consider solely money costs then such modes as bus (if available) or car will have costs which are increasing functions of distance. Moreover the relation between cost and distance is likely to vary between modes. Assuming that the shopping cost element (τ) is the same for all modes then for a particular type of case the costs of both will rise with distance, probably with a substantial initial cost and then with a fairly flat marginal cost per mile. For the bus the minimum cost is that of travelling one stop, which is usually high relative to the costs of travelling additional stops. For a car there are several costs involved; not only is there the cost of petrol and of the wear on the car, but often there is also the more substantial cost of parking. Hence we might characterize a typical consumer as facing money cost schedules as shown in Figure 7.1. We have assumed a higher fixed cost but lower marginal cost for the use of a car. Clearly, at distances below t^* it would be cheaper to take the bus while at greater distances the car would be cheaper. Of course the 'fixed cost' element for the car must include any parking charge, and the greater this is the further the switch point would be from the centre.

Calculations of this type are in fact fairly straightforward to establish. However, it is clear that the pure money cost approach can say nothing about the two other transport modes often encountered (foot and bicycle), nor does it do full justice to the factors influencing a consumer in the choice between car and bus. For

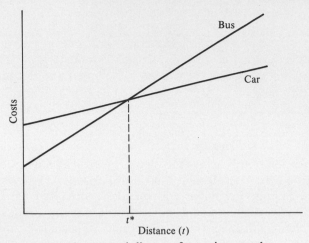

Fig. 7.1 Money travel costs and distance for various modes

modes with no direct financial cost, we are forced to conclude that there must be some non-financial cost involved or else they would always be used whatever the circumstances. We see that there are in fact two cases to explain, which concern modes that have no monetary cost. First, there is the case of the shopper who lives fairly close to a centre but is connected by bus (perhaps only one stop away) and owns a car. Nevertheless, shoppers in this position often walk to the shops. On the other hand, shoppers in a similar position but living further away from the centre do not walk but use a mode which involves a money cost. Clearly there is some cost involved which is low for a short walk but high for a longer walk. In Chapter 2, in our discussion of the determinants of frequency, we pointed out that there can be 'implicit' costs involved in the travel to a centre. Time taken in travelling has an opportunity cost, and since different modes are slower or faster this cost will at any distance be different. Since we can take the average speed of a mode not to vary with distance, it follows that the 'time cost' of travel is strictly proportional to distance and that the constant of proportionality is different for different modes. Figure 7.2 illustrates a hypothetical set of 'time costs' for the three modes. Even if the relationships are not exactly linear, the basic feature is that the time costs of the modes are likely to be consistently ordered with respect to distance. At the same time there is no fixed cost element involved (except perhaps for the

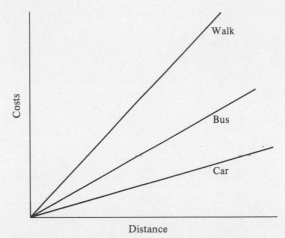

Fig. 7.2. Time travel costs and distance for various modes

average waiting time to catch a bus). If time costs alone were important then consumers would always travel by car and never walk, or travel by bus, whatever distance they lived from the shopping centre. However, the combination of time costs and money costs produces a more complex picture in which different modes might be chosen at different distances. Figure 7.3 shows one possible plausible set of total cost functions. We can see that there are two switch points, one at t^* where consumers switch from walking to using the bus, and then a second at t^{**} where they switch from bus to car. It is also possible (depending on the relative costs) that nobody would use the bus—they either walk or use the car—and the lower the fixed costs of the car the more likely this would be.

This analysis shows that different consumers will choose different modes depending on distance and availability. However, in this model a given consumer will always use the same mode on trips to a given centre. To anticipate our discussion of modal choice in the two-centre case, however, we can see that a consumer might well visit both centres and use different modes to do so. If the distances to the two centres were unequal (but were such that using both was optimal) the modes chosen could well be different even though the same choice was available for trips to both centres.

The ideas developed earlier for the cost-minimizing model are reinforced when we look at a utility-maximizing model. In Chapter 2 we presented a model (f) where the consumer placed a value on the

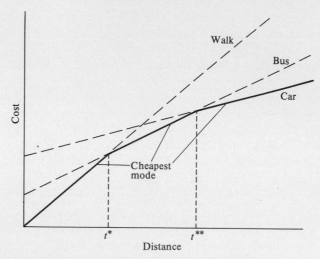

Fig. 7.3. Total travel costs and distance for various modes

time available for leisure. Hence time taken over shopping not only lowered income but also reduced leisure. It was shown, for example, where the utility function was of the form

$$U = (qf)^\alpha L \qquad (7.4)$$

with budget constraints

$$wH = pqf + cpq + tf \qquad (7.5)$$

$$L = T - H - S \qquad (7.6)$$

$$S = fb \qquad (7.7)$$

where

w = hourly wage rate,
H = number of hours working,
L = number of hours leisure,
S = number of hours shopping,
b = time taken shopping per trip,

that optimal frequency and bundle size were functions of all the parameters. Utility at the optimum declines with both t (the money cost and transport) and b (the time taken to shop). Clearly, since b and t will vary between modes there is a possibility that at different distances the modal choice will vary. The model in effect introduces a total cost of a trip ($t^* = wb + t$) so that at any given distance the mode with the lowest t^* will be chosen. Hence if different modes have the lowest t^* at different distances, modal choice will vary with distance. Our analysis for the cost-minimizing model concentrated on these two costs, but in an informal fashion, but we see that exactly similar conclusions will be reached and that the switches in mode will occur at exactly the same distances from the centre.

In Chapter 2 utility functions were also generalized in order to consider the possibility that there is an inherent disutility in shopping— namely the difficulty of carrying the shopping. Case (g) took utility as

$$U = Kq^\gamma f \tag{7.8}$$

with a budget constraint

$$Y = pqf + cpq + tf \tag{7.9}$$

$$\gamma = (1 - \beta\alpha)/(1 - \alpha) \tag{7.10}$$

where α is proportional to the disutility of carrying the goods and K involves both a distance factor and a mode factor. The higher the distance and the less attractive the mode, the lower will be K. This structure would have very similar predictions to the others if disutility of mode were related to the implicit cost of using the mode. Since it is not unrealistic to argue that the slow modes are also the least pleasant to use for heavy shopping, it seems that this force also pushes the consumer to the use of car first, then bus, and lastly foot. On the other hand the pure financial cost element remains as before, so that the prediction is exactly as in the two previous cases. Near to a centre the consumer will walk, further away the bus will be used, and finally the car will be used. In certain conditions the bus will not be used at all.

So far all models generate a single choice of mode for a given centre and never predict that different modes could be used to the same centre on different occasions. We next consider an important case in which multi-modal choice to a given centre is possible even in the single-good case.

SHOPPING WITH RESTRICTED MODAL AVAILABILITY

One of the most important features of family shopping is the regular, but not necessarily very frequent, shopping trip made by car to a major shopping centre. Often this possibility is restricted to week-end shopping because that is the only time the car is available for that purpose. These once-a-week (say) trips may well be to a centre used on other occasions during the week, but with a different mode. Often, however, they will be to a centre not otherwise utilized. The possibility of limited availability of the family car may, then, affect the pattern of shopping considerably.

If we consider the cost-minimizing fixed value model in the single-good case the unrestricted optimum is where

$$TC^* = V + 2\sqrt{(cVt)}. \tag{7.11}$$

If there is no mode restriction then that mode with the smallest t is chosen. However, if a mode has only a limited availability then the analysis will have to be extended. Clearly, if the restricted mode would not be chosen even were it to be freely available, then there would be no effect on the analysis. However, suppose mode 1 is preferred ($t_1 < t_i$ all $i \neq 1$) for the given consumer, then the optimal number of trips (f^*) may not be feasible. Generally,

$$f^*_1 = \sqrt{(cV/t_1)}. \tag{7.12}$$

If the availability of mode 1 is denoted by $\bar{f}_1$ and

$$\bar{f}_1 < f^*_1$$

then equation (7.12) is not feasible. In general the choice of optimum frequency is complex in this case, particularly because the bundle size might be thought to vary between the different types of trip. This would imply a different interval between successive utilizations of the two different modes and it might well turn out that the model would predict larger bundles to be purchased on the trips restricted as to mode. The possibility of unequal bundle size, even though of some interest, increases the difficulty of analysis very greatly, as we saw in Chapter 3, and so we illustrate these arguments with our simple three-cost model using the restrictive assumption of equal bundle size irrespective of the mode chosen. The cost functions are

$$TC = V + cV/f + t_1 f \tag{7.13}$$

for $f < \bar{f}$ (where $\bar{f}$ is the restricted availability of mode 1, which we call 'car'), and

$$TC^* = V + cV/f + t_1 \bar{f} + t_2 (f - \bar{f}) \tag{7.14}$$

for $f \geq \bar{f}$. The first cost function is fixed but terminates at the truncation point $\bar{f}$, while the second function changes in shape and shifts with the truncation point.

There are three aspects to notice of these functions:

(i) $TC = TC^*$ at $\bar{f}$.
(ii) The first function has a single minimum

$$\hat{f} = \sqrt{(CV/t_1)} \tag{7.15}$$

and the second has its (infeasible) minimum

$$\check{f} = \sqrt{(CV/t_2)}. \tag{7.16}$$

(iii) $TC^* > TC$ for $f > \bar{f}$ (since $t_2 > t_1$).

The functions can be drawn as shown in (a), (b), and (c) in Figure 7.4. The first case, (a), has the unrestricted optimum $\hat{f}$ lower than the restriction. The restricted optimum is lower still, but it is not feasible. Hence the consumer is not affected by the restriction and is able to use the car as much as he desires. Case (b) has the unrestricted optimum larger than the restriction, while the restricted optimum is smaller. Again, $C^* > C$ in the region feasible for C^*. The consumer then would ideally like to use the car more but cannot do so, and does not use any of the higher transport cost trips to increase the frequency of shopping. In case (c) the unrestricted and restricted

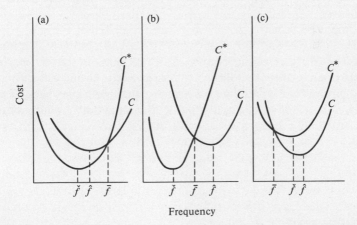

Fig. 7.4. Frequency and costs of shopping when there is a restriction on modal availability

optima are greater than the value of the restriction so, although $C^* > C$ in this region, the best value is not to stick to the restriction $\bar{f}$ (using just the car whenever available) but to make some trips on the more expensive mode (say the 'bus'). There is not, however, full compensation for the restriction ($\check{f} < \bar{f}$). Hence for a given consumer we can plot frequency and modal choice against the value of the restrictions, as in Figure 7.5. The 45° line shows where total frequency is equal to availability. For availability below $\bar{f} = \sqrt{(CV/t_2)}$

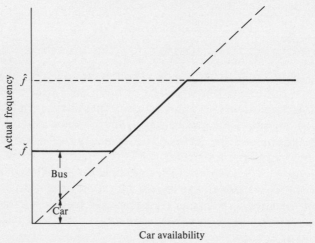

Fig. 7.5. Frequency and modal choice as functions of the degree of car availability

the shopper will use both modes and will use the bus ($\bar{f} - \check{f}$) times. For availability between $\check{f}$ and $\hat{f} = \sqrt{(CV/t_1)}$ the shopper will use the car as often as possible (subject to the restriction) but will not use the bus, and for availability greater than $\hat{f}$ the car will not be used on every occasion that it is available. Similar qualitative conclusions can be derived from a utility-maximizing framework and from models which allow for variable bundle size.

This analysis can be subjected to the normal parametric variations. As the requirements rise (V), perhaps because income is rising, both optima rise but the value of $\hat{f}$ rises by a larger absolute amount than $\check{f}$. Hence over a wider range of availability there will be multimodal shopping programmes.

An even more interesting variation is to consider what happens as distance increases (i.e. as we consider identical consumers living further away from the shopping centre). We begin by assuming that the restricted mode (car) is cheaper than the alternative mode (bus) at every distance from the city centre, so that without restrictions on availability all consumers would use only the car. There is, however, a restriction $(\bar{f})$ on car availability. For all consumers for whom $\hat{f} < \bar{f}$ the restriction is non-binding and this means that for all consumers living beyond a distance $\bar{t}$, obtained from solving

$$\bar{f} = \sqrt{\{cV/t_1(\bar{t})\}}, \tag{7.17}$$

the restriction does not bind (where $t_1(\bar{t})$ is the cost of travelling distance t on mode 1). Hence for those living beyond $\bar{t}$ the car is always used. Similarly, for consumers living nearer to the centre than a distance t^0, obtained from solving

$$\bar{f} = \sqrt{\{cV/t_2(t^0)\}}, \tag{7.18}$$

it will be optimal to use the car whenever available and also to use the bus on the rest of the desired trips indicated by equation (7.16). Between these two distances consumers use only the car but would increase the number of shopping trips if it were more frequently available.

We can also see that 'improvements' in the bus service (i.e. reducing t_2 towards t_1) will increase the use of buses by increasing frequency of usage from those already using the bus and by extending the range at which some use of the bus is optimal. On the other hand, if t_2 is very high with respect to t_1 very little use will be made of mode 2.

Finally, it is possible to combine the two themes presented here by analysing the case where different modes would dominate at various distances together with restrictions on the availability of certain modes. We can do this by considering the three-mode model (car, bus, foot) with transport cost functions which are of the type given earlier in this chapter. We argued that closest to the centre everyone would walk. Further out the bus would be used, and beyond that the car would be used. There would be two switch points t^* and t^{**} (distances from the centre) where mode changed. The restriction on the car produces a series of possible results. Let us call the distances of the optima of the two car cost functions $\hat{t}$ (with no restrictions) and $\check{t}$ (with a restriction). It depends on where these come in relation to t^{**}. If $\check{t}$ is greater than t^{**} the bus is used as well as the car in this zone. If $t < \check{t}^{**}$ (while $\hat{t} > t^{**}$) then there are some consumers who would use the car more if possible (but there are no consumers using two modes). Finally, if $\hat{t} < t^{**}$ then there are no effective restrictions on consumer behaviour (and no multi-mode shopping programmes). Hence the bus may be used entirely in a zone where it is economically preponderant and also partly in a more distant zone where limited car availability pushes consumers to use the alternative mode.

This analysis has been carried out without imposing the integrality constraints that we have argued are essential for the understanding of multi-centre shopping. It would be possible to repeat the previous analysis but making sure that only integer solutions were chosen. The nature of the results would not change, except if $\hat{f}$ and $\bar{f}$ were sufficiently close there might not be an integer value solution between them and so multi-modal shopping need not always occur. It will certainly still be optimal under certain cost conditions.

We next turn to considerations of modal choice and market area when there is more than one centre but still only one good. This raises in elementary form the problem of simultaneous choice over mode and allocation.

ALLOCATION AND MODAL CHOICE FOR THE TWO-CENTRE ONE-GOOD CASE

The extension of the previous analysis to the two-centre case presents no difficulties if all consumers have the same choice of transport modes to each centre. The analysis of Chapter 1 shows that whatever the mode considered consumers prefer the nearer centre and so the market boundary is half-way between the centres. If the centres were sufficiently close it could mean that certain modes were never chosen. The car might become the cheapest mode at distances over 1 mile, but if the two centres were only 1½ miles apart then no consumer would live more than ¾ mile from any centre and the car would never be used.

The interesting cases occur when the transport opportunities are not symmetric. We can imagine, for example, that one centre is served by a bus which connects only with certain parts of the town, while the other centre has no public transport. In the simplest case, where the bus is cheaper than walking at all distances, then clearly all those living nearer to B than to A will go to B and travel by bus. In addition, since the cost to B is less per unit distance, there will be a point nearer to A at which the consumer is indifferent between bus to B or walking to A. However, it would never pay to extend the route beyond a certain point. Once we complicate the analysis by introducing the notion that at certain distances it is cheaper to walk than to take the bus then the trade using the bus is limited. Let a distance (δ) be the distance at which a bus becomes superior. If the distance between the centres is less than 2δ then the bus to centre B (or to centre A) would do no trade. The success of the bus clearly depends on the spacing of the centres and the modal switch distance between walking and using the bus. For greater distances we have argued that a car would be superior to a bus, so that even for centres very far apart there is a maximum trade the bus could capture. An important feature of the asymmetrical provision of transport is the likely result that the catchment areas of the two centres, which are equivalent in other respects, will be different.

An important related aspect of such models is not only the question of the equilibrium location of centres but also that of the equilibrium provision of public transport. In the single-good two-centre case with population spread homogeneously along the linear town, the incentives to provide transport for either centre are the same and in a full equilibrium model provision of transport is likely to be equal. Once we move to hierarchical structures (or non-uniform population densities) this need no longer be the case. With differential transport facilities the degree of success of centres will differ and so the effect of this on the provision of public transport may reinforce an existing tendency towards inequality between centres.

MODAL CHOICE IN THE TWO-GOOD ONE-CENTRE CASE

In the straightforward case where, for any given consumer, a particular mode is always cheapest there is no new problem associated with the two-good case. The consumer decides which mode and then optimizes his shopping pattern accordingly. Even if he has a mixed frequency programme, sometimes buying one good and sometimes buying two, the mode used on both types of trip is the same since it will be cheaper however many goods are purchased.

If there were a restriction on modal availability (i.e. in the frequency of travel by car) then this would be used up to the maximum number of occasions and extra trips made by the less preferred mode. An important feature of this model is that there is nothing to determine whether the car would preferentially be used for single-purpose or multi-purpose trips. This is not very satisfactory since intuition would suggest that the car would be saved for the trips on which the largest amount of shopping was done. The disutility factor of heavy bundles could discriminate between modes. It is also possible, as our analysis in the one-good case showed, that restrictions and modal availability would affect the frequencies. This might occur to such an extent that a situation of differential frequencies in the unrestricted model became equal frequencies in the restricted model.

MODAL CHOICE IN THE MANY-CENTRE MANY-GOOD FIXED FREQUENCY CASE

The model of Chapter 5 assumed that each centre could be indexed by its transport cost for a given consumer. With multi-modal availability we would merely take the cheapest transport cost to each centre between the competing modes and optimize for these costs. Further, if availability were the same for every consumer with respect to every centre then market areas could be determined, although the determination would be more complex since transport costs would no longer be a homogeneous linear function of distance. The various switching points could be determined as a function of transport costs and these could then be translated into modal choices at the various distances (since Figure 7.3 suggests that there is a unique mode distance for each transport cost). The model would be solved by the parametric programme as the distance cost parameter (t) was varied. Let us suppose that for consumers living between the two centres A and B, the critical aspect is how the cost functions vary with the distance parameter. If the costs were such that one mode dominates another at every distance then the problem reduces to a single-mode model. If the cost functions do not have this property then they cannot be linear homogeneous functions. There must be a more complex relation between cost and distance. We have argued that this is caused by a fixed charge element on some modes, for example:

cost of mode 1 at distance $t = d_1(t) = \alpha_1 t$ (for walking),
cost of mode 2 at distance $t = d_2(t) = \beta_0 + \beta_1 t$ with $\beta_1 < \alpha_1$.

The generalized shopping programme now defines each type of trip on a given mode as a separate activity. Hence in the two-centre, two-good, two-mode case there are the following:

f_{11} = trip to centre A to buy both goods on mode f,
f_{10} = trip to centre A to buy good 1 on mode f,
f_{01} = trip to centre A to buy good 2 on mode f,
f_{22} = trip to centre B to buy goods on mode f,
f_{20} = trip to centre B to buy good 1 on mode f,
f_{02} = trip to centre B to buy good 2 on mode f,
g_{ij} is defined analogously for trips by mode g.

Of course for any consumer most of these activities will not be used. But at different distances from the two centres not only will the combinations of goods and choice of centres vary but so also will the mode utilized. Hence for a consumer living at a distance t from centre A and at a distance $(\Delta - t)$ from centre B the programme is, minimize

$$f_{11}(t + p_{11} + p_{12}) + f_{10}(\alpha t + p_{11}) + f_{01}(\alpha t + p_{12})$$
$$+ g_{11}(\beta_0 + \beta_1 t + p_{11} + p_{12}) + g_{10}(\beta_0 + \beta_1 t + p_{11}) + g_{01}(\beta_0 + \beta_1 t + p_{12})$$
$$+ f_{22}(\alpha\{\Delta - t\} + p_{22} + p_{21}) + f_{20}(\alpha\{\Delta - t\} + p_{21}) + f_{02}(\alpha\{\Delta - t\} + p_{22})$$
$$+ g_{22}(\beta_0 + \beta_1\{\Delta - t\} + p_{22} + p_{11}) + g_{20}(\beta_0 + \beta_1\{\Delta - t\} + p_{21}) +$$
$$g_{02}(\beta_0 + \beta_1\{\Delta - t\} + p_{22}) \qquad (7.19)$$

subject to

$$f_{11} + f_{10} + g_{11} + g_{10} + f_{22} + f_{20} + g_{22} + g_{20} = m_1$$
$$f_{11} + f_{01} + g_{11} + g_{01} + f_{22} + f_{02} + g_{22} + g_{02} = m_2, \qquad (7.20)$$

all variables integer.

With two restrictions only two activities will be used, as before, but there is a possibility that these will be by different modes. Of course for any single consumer it is computationally much simpler to identify the cheaper mode for a journey to either centre and then restrict the problem to activities using the cheaper mode. This would of course halve the number of variables immediately. However, for the parametric programme which is used to optimize over each consumer in turn and hence to identify market boundaries, it is perhaps preferable to work with the problem stated in this general form. There is clearly no simple pattern to the set of solutions. Depending on the relative prices at the two centres and on the two transport cost functions, it may be either that all consumers use the same mode to a centre or that different consumers use different modes. It is clear that for any one consumer all trips to a given centre will be by the same mode. It also seems clear that the selection of transport modes available can affect the market areas of the two centres.

If there is a restricted availability of a particular mode (for example the use of a car) then it is easy in the preceding programming model to introduce such a constraint. Let the total number of trips per unit period by mode g be not greater then K. Hence we must add the inequality restriction

$$g_{11} + g_{10} + g_{01} + g_{22} + g_{20} + g_{02} \leq K. \qquad (7.21)$$

This clearly presents no extra analytical problem since it conforms to the standard linear programme, and for integer values of K the optimal values will continue to be integer. We can see that if this constraint binds, three activities will be used, and this implies that two different modes of transport to the same centre will be utilized. Further insights into shopping patterns with respect to both mode and centre choice as affected by changes in car availability can be obtained by solving the linear programme parametrically for variations in K.

We can also vary the cost coefficients α and β to show how allocations and modal choice will change as relative costs change. Using the double-description technique we could simultaneously vary a transport cost element (for example β_0) and distance t so as to obtain a locus of the solution boundaries with respect to distance as the fixed cost element of mode g alters.

Clearly, within the limitations placed by the fixed frequency assumption the multi-mode cost-minimizing model is capable of answering a number of interesting questions.

MODAL CHOICE IN THE TWO-CENTRE TWO-GOOD VARIABLE FREQUENCY CASE

The most refined model of consumer behaviour that we have considered is the cost-minimizing allocation problem when there are two goods and two centres (subject to fixed value requirements). This model is now investigated in the case where there is more than one transport mode available.

Chapter 6 has shown how the choice between centres in the single-mode case turns out to be very simple. If both centres sell both goods then the boundary between the centres is where the transport cost of a trip to either centre is equal. Hence if all modes are equally available at both centres then the cost functions with respect to distance will be the same and the boundary will be half-way between the centres. Of course for the trips to a given centre the mode can vary with distance, as before (see the single-centre two-good case). This relationship can be solved separately from the problem of allocation and so no new problems arise. In fact all the analysis has the same characteristics as the two-centre one-good case.

Once we turn to the hierarchical structure of shopping centres the situation is more complex, even when modal availability is the same everywhere. Chapter 6 showed that all consumers for whom the transport cost to the higher-order centre was less than that to the lower-order centre would do all their shopping at the higher-order centre. This will remain true irrespective of the availability of various modes. However, for certain parameter combinations those living nearer (in a transport cost sense) to the lower-order centre will not use that centre as well as using the higher-order centre for multi-purpose shopping trips. The boundary between those consumers and those who used both centres depended in part on the relative transport costs and in part on the pure shopping cost (τ). Also, the boundary can depend on the value requirement, as equation (6.27) indicated. The position of this boundary, which is not symmetric between the centres even in the single-mode case, will be affected by the range of modes available and the cost curves associated with them. The boundary in cost terms will still be given by the same equation but its location will vary depending on the relation of transport cost to distance (Figure 7.3). Hence, as we change the magnitude of transport costs relative to shopping and purchase costs, or the relative costs of the two modes, the boundary will shift (unlike the case where both centres provide both goods). Market areas will change, so that in the case of hierarchical structures the general level of transport costs as well as their relative costs, even in the case of uniform availability, will play an important role in determining market areas. For example, the results of Chapter 6 show that the boundary between a programme of shopping once per time period for both goods at centre A and a programme of once a week to A for both goods and once a week to centre B for good 1 is

$$t_A = t_B - \tau + 2cV_1 \qquad (7.22)$$

providing that $2cV_1 > \tau$. (For Γ less than 14 this is clearly the boundary between single-centre shopping and multi-centre shopping.) For our parameters of $\tau = 1$ and $cV_1 + 4$ we have

$$t_A - t_B = 7$$

(where t_A and t_B are the transport costs to the two centres). Figure 7.6 shows how the boundary is related to transport costs. We plot dis-

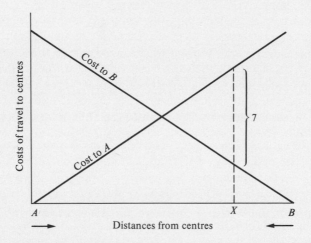

Fig. 7.6. Market boundaries and transport cost functions for a hierarchy and a single transport mode

tance against costs from centre A running to the right and the same from centre B running to the left. If there is a single mode of transport with a linear homogeneous cost schedule then for our parameter values the boundary is where the cost of travel to A is 7 more than the cost of travel to B (assuming the centres are not too far distant in cost terms). Clearly, changes in transport cost alter the location of the boundary (multiplying both costs by a factor λ will shift the boundary towards A if $\lambda > 1$). A multi-mode cost model is shown in Figure 7.7.

Given uniform availability the modal switchpoint occurs at the same distance from each centre. Again, the boundary is where the cost of travel to A is 7 greater than the cost to B. It is obvious that changes in the relative costs of the two modes as well as in transport

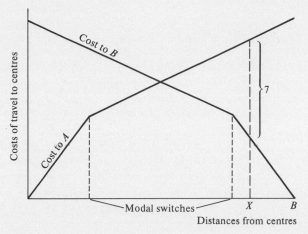

Fig. 7.7. Market boundaries and transport cost functions for a hierarchy and two transport modes

costs to the other costs will affect the market boundary. In our example the consumers at X are indifferent between using a car to centre A (once a week for both goods) and using the car to A once a week for both goods plus making one trip on foot to B for good 1 (bundle sizes for good 1 being altered accordingly). An increase in car costs would push up the higher section of the cost curves and the boundary would shift towards A, hence increasing the amount of trade going to the lower-order centre. This example does show that allocation and modal choice may be simultaneously determined in the hierarchical case.

SHOPPING TRIPS AND NON-SHOPPING ACTIVITIES

All the discussion and analysis so far has concentrated on the case where the shopper begins the trip at home, visits a centre solely for the purpose of shopping, and then returns home again. Although much shopping activity does fit this pattern, it is well known that there are two important deviations from it. Shopping is often done from the place of work (particularly during lunch-breaks or after work has finished) and often trips from the home to the centre are combined with some non-shopping activity. Both of these cases can be treated in the same fashion. In both cases the consumer has to go to the centre for another reason and thus the additional cost of travel to the centre in order to shop will be zero. Hence in any time period the consumer will have available a certain number of trips with no travel cost. If the place of work is at a higher-order centre it should be possible for the consumer to do all the required shopping on those trips. Visits to libraries will perhaps permit only part of the total requirement to be carried out. Indeed the attractiveness of the possibility of shopping at the place of work seems so strong that we need to consider why it might be that such people would do any other shopping. The two restrictions that seem to be relevant are first, a limitation on the amount of time available, when working, while the shops are still open and second, the disinclination to carry large volumes of shopping if the car is not used for the journey to work. In the case of non-shopping activities which could be carried out at a series of locations there is the problem of choosing a location which makes best use of the possibility of 'joint-purpose' trips. If we were to treat the visit to the library as a fixed value requirement for a hypothetical good, with the centres being indexed by the provision of libraries as well as by the provision of goods, then we can see that higher-order centres with libraries will tend to attract shopping trade from people who would not otherwise have gone there. We can imagine in our two-good, two-centre example that the higher-order good is the provision of a library. The boundary for the purchase of the lower-order good (the actual shopping) is not half-way between the centres (which are identical in terms of the range of shops provided) but is displaced towards the lower-order centre, as we have shown in Chapter 6. Hence a non-uniform provision of non-shopping activities effectively creates a hierarchical-type structure which increases the trade going to the shop at the higher-order centres.

These last two points will reinforce the tendency that this model has to produce hierarchical structures. Larger shopping centres will tend to create more jobs and thus to generate more trade from place of work. At the same time non-shopping activities are often located at the higher-order centres because they are visited by more people. Both factors will increase the success of the higher-order centre and reduce the trade going to lower-order centres. The tendency of the system towards hierarchy may be strengthened by these related factors.

CONCLUSION

The analysis sketched in this chapter does suggest that the deterministic model of location decisions developed earlier in the book can be generalized to take account of certain features of the transport opportunities available to individual consumers. The use of different modes to travel to different centres can occur when there is a hierarchy, and when the consumer is restricted in the use of a given mode (usually car travel) the model shows how different modes can be chosen for various trips to the same centre.

Once we turn to the differences between consumers we see that distance to a centre can affect the choice of mode and, in certain cases, that the availability of modes will affect which centre is chosen.

The existence of joint-purpose trips generated by the need to visit a centre for a non-shopping activity can affect where shopping is done and hence the market area for the centre in question.

Variations in the public provision of transport facilities and of non-shopping activities can have strong effects on the shopping patterns within a town.

8

RETROSPECT AND PROSPECT

In the introduction we argued that in the study of urban economics there are a number of 'stylized facts' or 'empirical regularities' that characterize the location patterns of shops and the shopping behaviour of individuals, and that existing theories and models of behaviour are inadequate to explain such patterns. The models are either exclusively for the study of one good or are purely statistical in nature, or else they are based on assumptions about consumer behaviour that are manifestly untrue. These observations define the target for this study—a theory that has a minimum requirement certain properties. The theory has to be applicable to more than one good and has to have the possibility of predicting that:

   (i) not all goods need be purchased at the same frequency;
 (ii) there can be some multi-purpose shopping trips on which more than one good is bought at a shopping centre;
(iii) not all purchases of a good need be made at the nearest centre selling the good;
 (iv) some goods can be purchased, on different shopping trips, at different centres.

The abandoning of the 'single-purpose trip' hypothesis and the 'nearest centre trip' hypothesis may help to produce a model with more realistic consumer behaviour, but such a model also needs to be consistent with the existence of hierarchical-type structures of shopping centres. Such structures, one of the key predictions of central place and other related theories, are the goal of most location theories and are seen as essential constraints on the class of model that is acceptable.

We began by studying a rather neglected aspect of shopping behaviour—that of the frequency of shopping. Many factors can affect the frequency of purchase, even in the case of a single good, and we were able to show how not only the money cost involved but also the opportunity costs in terms of leisure or the disutility of shopping might be incorporated into a systematic treatment of frequency. However, the central idea, running throughout this part of the book, was that there are two opposing forces which are balanced against each other in the determination of the optimal frequency. On the one hand, the costs of holding a large inventory of shopping, associated with interest foregone, losses due to perishability, space constraints, etc., push the consumer towards frequent shopping. On the other hand, the 'order' costs of shopping, both the money costs of transport and the time costs of shopping itself, push the consumer towards infrequent shopping. Any model with these two forces is likely to produce a finite optimum for the frequency of shopping. In the single-good case we showed, however, that the model with transport cost structure in which order costs are proportional to the amount purchased on a trip produces a zero bundle size/infinite frequency solution. This result ruled out the use of generalizations based on Hotelling's (1929) model to the many-good case. It was thus shown that, as well as the two forces, it is necessary to adopt certain structures of transport costs in order to obtain usable results.

The simplest possible model which embodied these features was then developed for the two-good case. The critical requirement for such a model is the establishment of the possibility that the frequencies of purchase of the two goods at the optimum can be different even though all shopping were done at a single centre. The development of a model which produces this result was shown to be possible. The key to producing this type of behaviour is in the structure of the order cost element of shopping. If the purely centre-specific element (travel cost) dominates, then all trips are multi-purpose and all frequencies are equal. This result does not permit hierarchical structures to emerge even though it is consistent with the emergence of the highest order of centre. At the other extreme, if the purely good-specific element (shopping cost) dominates then there are no multi-purpose trips and all shopping is done at the nearest source of supply. Only a model which allows for both elements can produce the possibility of differential frequencies together with some multi-purpose trips. It was shown how optimal combinations of frequencies could be identified for a model with this order cost structure. In order to solve this optimization problem a special algorithm was developed because the essentially discontinuous nature of the cost function (depending on whether or not trips were multi-purpose) rules out the use of standard calculus techniques. The simple structure of the objective function (the total costs of shopping per period) plays a crucial role in allowing a set of rules to be developed which can check whether any given frequency combination is optimal or not. As a result of this analysis it was shown that optimal frequencies can be different for a given consumer, but that they are not necessarily so for all consumers. In particular, it was shown that over substantial variations in distance from the centre the shopping patterns are the same.

Once the possibility of the key differential frequency result was established for the single-centre case, attention was shifted to the modelling of the choice of location for purchasing in the many-centre many-good case. Although little work had been done on this, it was clear from earlier work that the key to choice of location lies in the assumptions made about frequency. Accordingly, a model with predetermined but differential frequencies was investigated for the many-centre case. By casting the model in a form suitable for treatment by linear programming techniques, it was possible to show how the allocation problem can be solved even when optimal values are restricted to integers. Such a model is capable of predicting both that some trips are multi-purpose, and that they need not be made to the nearest source of supply. The transport cost structure of such a model pays attention only to the centre-specific elements of order costs but it was shown that, in the fixed frequency case, the shopping cost element cannot affect allocation. It was next shown how to obtain the market areas of the centres and shops by using the techniques of parametric programming to identify all consumers, indexed by the distances to the shopping centres, who have the same optimal allocation of shopping trips. The combined effect of these last two steps was to permit the construction of the total demand going to a centre, given the allocations of all other shops. Furthermore, it was shown to be likely that this demand can be systematically related to the location of the shop in question. Once a demand 'curve' of this type is constructed then a full supply/demand equilibrium seems feasible.

The two principal themes of the book, choice over frequency and choice over location, were integrated in Chapter 6, where a model of their simultaneous choice was presented. Certain special features of the model used (in particular the fixed value assumptions) permitted a particularly straightforward analysis in the two-good two-centre case. If the centres are arranged in a hierarchical pattern it was shown that the higher-order centre attracts some of the trade in the good sold at both centres from consumers living nearer to the lower-order centre. Indeed, if the lower-order centre locates too close to the higher-order centre it may attract no trade at all. These results are the confirmation that the model of frequency determination is consistent with multi-purpose and non nearest-neighbour shopping, and accordingly it seems likely to be consistent with the existence of hierarchical equilibrium structures of shopping centres.

The analysis of individual consumer behaviour was taken further by analysing the effects of the existence of several modes (and costs) of transport for a given location. It was shown that the model can generate a prediction of the use of different modes to different centres for certain consumers when there is a hierarchy of centres, and can even predict the use of more than one mode to a given centre if there is a restriction on the frequency of use of the most popular mode. Furthermore, in the hierarchical case the availability or not of the various modes determines, for some consumers, which centre is chosen. The result, coupled with that aspect of the model which relates choice of mode to the distance from a centre, suggests that the question of the optimal public provision of transport could be investigated in models of this type. All these results on modal choice were derived for a deterministic model of individual behaviour rather than for a stochastic model of aggregate behaviour of the type that usually characterizes investigations into travel behaviour. Further insights into the possibilities of the model were obtained from considering the choice of shopping locations once journey to work or journeys for non-shopping purposes were considered. Both of these factors seem likely to reinforce the attractions of the largest centres and will therefore tend to affect the equilibrium spacing of centres in the hierarchy.

This account of the ideas and results of this book makes clear what the next step in the use of the model should be. A model of supply should be constructed, most probably on the lines suggested by Eaton and Lipsey (1982), so that a general equilibrium could be derived. Even for the simplest two-good case in a small town (i.e. with few centres) this is likely to be a substantial undertaking. In particular, the rules governing the relocation of the shops (the 'conjectural variations' of oligopoly theory) are likely to be very important. The investigation of this problem, which combines location theory and oligopoly theory, is beyond the scope of a book devoted to the demand side of the problem, but is clearly needed before judgement can be passed on the ability of the type of model presented here to form the basis for a successful location model for shopping activities.

Once the approach has been justified there are several aspects of the model of consumer spatial behaviour which require further work to generalize the validity of the results, or which could be pursued in order to apply the model to a wider range of special cases.

The most obvious shortcoming of the two-good optimum shopping model is that it takes as its objective the minimization of total costs of shopping per period subject to purchasing given values of each good per period. To give the model the generality which is usually required in economics it would be necessary to construct a model, with a similar cost structure, in which total utility per period was maximized subject to an income constraint. Models of the latter sort give a role to price variations, both between goods and between centres. It would be interesting to model consumer behaviour in this more general context, although it is unlikely that the results for consumer behaviour would be qualitatively affected. Much more important would be the role of prices in an equilibrium model. The shape of the cost curves as well as the effect of prices on the quantity and location of demand could have a decisive influence on the nature of the equilibrium distribution of shops and shopping centres. However, to carry out this step it is not going to be possible to use the relatively straightforward algorithm developed in Chapter 3, and we can speculate that the integer non-linear programme that would be involved might be extremely difficult to solve except by purely enumerative methods.

The extension of the fixed value cost-minimizing model to larger numbers of goods is not likely to raise any new difficulties except that the number of solutions neighbouring each other is likely to rise substantially. Similarly, increases in the number of centres will not require the development of new methods but rather the repeated use of those already developed.

One development of the model that would be feasible is its extension in order to take account of individual family characteristics. All the analysis so far has distinguished households explicitly by their distance to the shopping centres, by the transport opportunities available, and by the value requirements for the different goods. At the same time shopping costs and travel costs are important elements in the model and those too could be related to household characteristics. The application of the model to various stages in the family 'life cycle' could produce substantial variations in shopping behaviour. We give a brief outline for five stages in the life cycle in order to show how the factors built into the model could be extended to allow systematically for variations in behaviour related to family structure.

(a) A newly married couple with both partners working

In families of this type, income might be at a medium level relative to requirements but non-working time would be scarce. There would, however, be plenty of opportunities for some joint-purpose shopping from the place of work. The low transport cost element together with the high frequency of such trips would greatly reduce the likelihood of shopping elsewhere, apart from speciality items or for unforeseen needs. In particular, little use is likely to be made of the nearest group of shops unless this also happens to be the place of work.

If, however, the time for joint-purpose trips is constrained, or neither partner works at or near a high-order shopping centre, then a different pattern would emerge, with the opportunity cost of free time being so high that the family is likely to make infrequent, multi-purpose trips and buy large bundles on such trips. The Friday-evening trip to a late-opening shopping centre or the Saturday trip to the town centre, particularly when a car is owned, would be an expected pattern. Inventory costs and shopping costs are likely to be unimportant relative to the time costs of travel, so that multi-purpose trips would predominate. Modal choice likewise will tend to be dominated by the need to visit high-order centres.

(b) A newly married couple with only one partner working

Income is likely to be lower than in case (a) but the opportunity cost of time is likely to be much less. Money shopping costs will be more important relative to time costs and so the shopper is likely to be prepared to travel to the shops more often and to use single-purpose trips. Local shops, where the cost of transport is low, will be more popular and the disutility of carrying heavy bundles could be reduced by making more frequent trips.

In utility-maximizing models price differentials could well attract this category of shopper to higher-order centres if they charged sufficiently low prices to compensate for any money transport costs that would be incurred in their use.

(c) Families with young children

In the case where one partner needs to spend a lot of time with the children and is accompanied by them on shopping trips, the costs of time taken over shopping rise greatly and the pressure to use the nearest shop increases. Indeed, frequent short trips seem to suit this category best because they can be combined with the joint purpose of taking children for a walk. At the same time the value of the requirement for basic goods is likely to rise and a once-a-week trip to a higher-order centre (when the other partner is free) may be common, particularly if the use of a car is possible.

(d) Families with children of school age

Although the total requirements are likely to rise still further the constraints on time (if only one partner works) will be greatly relaxed. The pattern may well switch away from frequent trips to the local shops to fewer trips but to more distant shops. This is likely to be reinforced by the possibility of making joint-purpose trips to undertake other activities in the larger centres.

(e) Retired families

In this case income has often fallen substantially even relative to requirements, and so the money costs of travel will be undesirable. At the same time the disutility both of long trips or of trips involving large bundles will tend to produce a high number of trips to the nearest centre (particularly if it is within walking distance).

These reflections on the possible relationships between family structure and the pattern of shopping serve to indicate how the analysis might be developed at an individual level. However, such considerations might also have implications for urban planning—a new housing estate built near a suburban shopping centre but with a few shops on the estate might well be a source of low demand for the centre if all the families who moved in were newly married and were therefore predominantly in category (c). Only when the next stage of demographic development was reached might there be a substantial shift of trade to the centre. Much later, when the average age of the estate had increased greatly, the trade might switch back to the local shops. Demographic shifts of this nature may have a part to play in explaining the varying success of a given location over time.

Other factors will also be important in understanding the shifting patterns of urban structure. Large shifts in transport costs or the value of time relative to other parameters might well direct trade away from lower-order centres, so that the range of the higher-order centre is increased (perhaps to the point where the lower-order centre is slowly forced out of the market).

Thus, although a good deal of work still needs to be done before it can be justifiably claimed that the model presented in this book can form the basis of an acceptable theory of urban retail location, there does already seem to be sufficient potential to warrant considerable optimism. Furthermore, the model seems capable of extension in a number of important and interesting fields.

BIBLIOGRAPHY

Ackley, G. (1941), 'Spatial Competition in a Discontinuous Market', *Quarterly Journal of Economics*, **56**, 212-30.

Bacon, R. W. (1968), *The Cowley Shopping Centre*, NEDO, HMSO, London.

Bacon, R. W. (1971), 'An Approach to the Theory of Consumer Shopping Behaviour', *Urban Studies*, **8**, 55-64.

Barten, A. P. (1977), 'The Systems of Consumer Demand Functions Approach: A Review', *Econometrica*, **45**, 23-51.

Becker, G. S. (1965), 'A Theory of the Allocation of Time', *Economic Journal*, **75**, 493-517.

Chiang, A. (1974), *Fundamental Methods of Mathematical Economics* (2nd edn.), McGraw Hill, Tokyo.

Christaller, W. (1966), *Central Places in Southern Germany* (translated by C. W. Buskin), Englewood Cliffs, New Jersey.

De Serpa, A. C. (1971), 'A Theory of the Economics of Time', *Economic Journal*, **81**, 829-46.

Eaton, B. C. and Lipsey, R. G. (1982), 'An Economic Theory of Central Places', *Economic Journal*, **92**, 56-72.

Engel, J. F., Kollat, D. T., and Blackwell, R. D. (1973), *Consumer Behaviour* (2nd edn.), Dryden Press, Illinois.

Evans, A. W. (1972), 'A Linear Programming Solution to the Shopping Problem Posed by R. W. Bacon', *Urban Studies*, **9**, 221-2.

Fetter, F. A. (1924), 'The Economic Law of Market Areas', *Quarterly Journal of Economics*, **38**, 520-29.

Gass, S. I. (1961), *Linear Programming: Methods and Applications* (3rd edn.), McGraw Hill, New York.

Gass, S. I. and Saaty, T. L. (1955), 'Parametric Objective Function (Part 2)—Generalisation', *Operations Research*, **3**, 395-401.

Hotelling, H. (1929), 'Stability in Competition', *Economic Journal*, **39**, 41-57.

Hoover, E. M. (1937), 'Spatial Price Discrimination', *Review of Economic Studies*, **4**, 182-91.

Hyson, C. D. and Hyson, W. P. (1950), 'The Economic Law of Market Areas', *Quarterly Journal of Economics*, **64**, 319-24.

Johnson, L. W. and Hensher D. A. (1979), 'A Random Coefficient Model of the Determinants of Frequency of Shopping Trips', *Australian Economic Papers*, **18**, 322-36.

Killen, J. (1983), *Mathematical Programming Methods for Geographers and Planners*, Croom Helm, London.

Lentenk, B., Harwitz, M., and Narula, S. C. (1981), 'Spatial Choice in Consumer Behaviour: Towards a Contextual Theory of Demand', *Economic Geography,* **57**, 362-72.

Lerner, A. P. and Singer, H. W. (1939), 'Some Notes on Duopoly and Spatial Competition', *Journal of Political Economy,* **45**, 145-86.

Lewis, W. A. (1945), 'Competition in Retail Trade', *Economica,* **12**, 202-34.

Naddor, E. (1966), *Inventory Systems,* Wiley, New York.

Odland, J. (1981), 'A Household Production Approach to Destination Choice', *Economic Geography,* **57**, 257-69.

Reilly, W. J. (1931), *The Law of Retail Gravitation,* Knickerbocker Press, New York.

Reinhardt, P. G. (1973), 'A Theory of Household Grocery Inventory Holdings', *Kyklos,* **26**, 497-511.

Saaty, T. L. and Gass, S. I. (1954), 'Parametric Objective Function (Part I), *Operations Research,* **2**, 316-19.

Schneider, E. (1935), 'Bemerkungen zu einer Theorie der Raumwirtschaft', *Econometrica,* **3**, 79-105.

Sharir, S. (1978), 'A Model of Households' Behaviour in Buying Frequently Purchased Goods', Research Paper 78-1, Department of Economics, University of Alberta.

Shepherd, I. D. and Thomas, C. J. (1980), 'Urban Consumer Behaviour', in *Retail Geography* (ed. J. A. Dawson), Croom Helm, London.

Smithies, A. (1941), 'Optimum Location in Spatial Competition', *Journal of Political Economy,* **49**, 423-39.

Wagner, H. M. (1969), *Principles of Operations Research,* Prentice Hall, New Jersey.

Zeuthen, F. (1933), 'Theoretical Remarks on Price Policy: Hotelling's Case with Variations', *Quarterly Journal of Economics,* **47**, 231-53.

INDEX

168

Index